CW00971476

THE BREWER'S TALE

THE BREWER'S TALE

A History of Ale in Yorkshire

Anthony Avis

The Radcliffe Press
London · New York

Published in 1995 by
The Radcliffe Press
45 Bloomsbury Square
London WC1A 2HY

175 Fifth Avenue
New York
NY 10010

In the United States of America
and Canada distributed by
St Martin's Press
175 Fifth Avenue
New York
NY 10010

A full CIP record for this book is available from the British Library

Library of Congress Catalog card number: 95–708045

A full CIP record is available from the Library of Congress

ISBN 1–86064–018–4

Copy-edited and laser-set by Selro Publishing Services, Oxford
Printed and bound in Great Britain by WBC Ltd, Bridgend, Mid Glamorgan

TO MY WIFE

Animo et Fide

Contents

Illustrations

Preface and Acknowledgements

This book is partly a summary and partly a rewritten set of brewery partners' diaries from 1879 to 1903. In addition to having to decipher the original authors' often obscure handwriting, it seemed necessary to give some explanation of what they were writing about and to provide a background to their observations. Some rather heavy editing has been required, for the accounts of their problems (which were multitude) and their triumphs (rather fewer) were often repeated.

I hope that this story of the establishment of a brewery in nineteenth century York, almost from scratch, by a group of young men from the titled classes unacquainted with the lower orders upon whom their prosperity depended, and their success, will be of interest to economic and social historians – further, it is a story about personal endeavour and human relationships.

That the diaries survived is a cause for wonder; for the first 50 years after their last entry they did so through a process of benign neglect – abandoned and forgotten in a cupboard. For the next 37 years they did so through my active custody of them. They are now in the care of the Bass brewery group, to whom I record my appreciation for being able to examine them again, and I am sure that, as the present custodians, they are aware of their value and will preserve them.

My first acknowledgement must be to a man who died 30 years ago; he was an antiquarian, an author of books on local history, and a bibliophile. As a very young man I was introduced to these diaries by him and they have fascinated me ever since. He was Harry Bradfer-Lawrence.

I also wish to acknowledge the assistance given to me by the staff of Bass PLC at its Leeds office, where I was given the chance to refresh my memory by inspecting the original diaries; the Local Studies Department of North Yorkshire County Council's York Library; and the National Monuments Record Department of the Royal Commission on the Historical Monuments of England, in respect of some of the illustrations appearing in this book. Last, I wish to thank Dr Lester Crook, of the Radcliffe Press, for guidance and professional help, and for whom the subject matter was a venture into strange territory.

A. A.

Introduction: The Travails of a Country Brewer

In 1875 the owners of the old-established business of Hotham & Company of George Street in York, William Hotham and his nephew Edward Hotham Newton, sold their interest in the brewery and its public houses to the new partners, Thomas Newton (E. H. Newton's brother), Russell Henry Monro and Frederick William Browne.

Little is known of them or their ability to run a brewery; Newton and Monro lived locally, and Browne in London. Only Monro, revealed in the diaries as young, impetuous, enquiring and quarrelsome, shows any capacity for management. Newton falls out with his partners and leaves the firm in circumstances that culminate in a legal action by him against the others, which ends in his penury. Browne seems to have been a sleeping partner only.

In 1877, standing in need of funds for the business, they admitted Henry Lloyd of Scarborough as a partner; he too seemed to have been quiescent and sold his share after five years.

Four years after they had embarked on this venture they must have come to the conclusion that they would either have to get bigger or get out. The opportunity arose to acquire some 50 more houses in the York area and, to raise the money for this purchase, they took in three new partners, Reginald Parker, Frederick Milner and John George Lambton.

They were all the younger sons of titled fathers and of an age requiring they should settle into careers that would combine leisure and moneymaking activities in proper measure, and be consonant with such natural and taught abilities as they might command. Since farming was in the doldrums for much of the nineteenth century and manufacturing industry required both energy and technical knowledge, brewing was the only option available both to meet their needs and accommodate their competence. The money for their shares was found by their families and it was clearly laid down that they were expected to run the business themselves. Milner already lived near York, Parker moved down from Newcastle-upon-Tyne and Lambton lived in County Durham.

With Monro they did in fact take on the running of the business and how they did it was recorded in their own handwriting in the office diaries they kept. They established their office in Hotham's brewery in George Street, and adopted a system of recording the affairs of a commercial undertaking that had been in use in all the European trading nations for many centuries.

A book was kept in the office and written into it were the facts, figures, hopes and fears of the proprietor or proprietors. A sole proprietor could use it as his *aide-mémoire*, account book, letter book and repository for his innermost thoughts, hopes and fears. A partnership could do the same, with the added precaution that all partners sign vital agreements and decisions as evidence of their assent. The book could be held securely under lock and key or it could be left open on the table in the partners' room. Anyone who has read the letters of the fourteenth-century merchant Francesco di Marco Datini, of the city of Prato in the plain of Florence in northern Italy, will know how vividly apposite still are the daily problems, joys and sorrows of a man trying to make a living, run a business and conduct his domestic life seven centuries ago.

In York in 1879, the three new partners came to the same conclusion as that merchant of long ago, namely that records had to be kept and communications established. Parker had done an apprenticeship in a bank and was well used to the partnership system, with office diaries and written records of all kinds. As soon as the new partners were admitted, he established the same system at York, writing the earliest entries himself, his style and the content of his entries showing the others the way.

There are ten volumes in all, covering the period from 1879 to 1903; the first is a hardboard notebook with lined quarto-sized sheets purchased from Johnson & Addeyman of Micklegate,

York. The second is quarto-sized, but otherwise similar, with the word 'DIARY', in typescript printed onto a piece of binding leather and obviously cut from an existing book, stuck on the front. Each of these volumes contains 150 pages. They roughly cover the first two years of the new partnership and are filled until the last page; there is no attempt to have one volume for each calendar year. Black ink is mostly used as the writing medium, though Monro occasionally resorted to red ink in his entries, plus underlining and exclamation marks when he was enraged. Sometimes pencil was used when interjecting comments, but never when inserting original notes. Entries were not made on a daily basis, but were nonetheless frequent and never more than a few days apart.

In 1882 the partners felt that a substantial and lasting diary should be used and Messrs Ben Johnson & Company of York were employed to make a strong board- and leather-bound volume, with an alphabetical index and the legend 'PARTNERS' DIARY', with the serial number, on the spine. The leaves were made of heavy quality paper and were numbered; within a few years there was a further change to books with a locking clasp made by John Lennox of Bond Street, Leeds, which continued through to 1903, the condition of these volumes being excellent to the present time.

After a desultory attempt to index entries in the 1882 volume, the facility was abandoned. The partners kept up the entries until the appointment of the first general manager, C. H. Tripp, in 1887 when, with an almost visible sigh of relief, they handed over to him the job of keeping the record, with just an occasional inserted comment. It was Tripp's vehicle for keeping the partners informed of his activities and obtaining their written approval of his actions, and their means of giving him instructions. There were no regular periodic meetings between them and their manager, nor were there any regular meetings between themselves; the diary was the only stable communication channel.

The system evolved from haphazard diary notes into planned meetings on a fixed timetable with an agenda of items for resolution, with those partners able to attend making the decisions, but it did not operate very smoothly. The reason for the locks on the diaries is not mentioned in the text and neither is there any indication of why the security of their contents was suddenly of importance. At some point, however, the keys to the locks must have been lost, for they are now all broken.

The diaries form a remarkable record of day-to-day happenings in a provincial brewery, with glimpses of life as it then was, with its problems and how those involved had to deal with them. The partners' comments reflect their characters, what they think of one another and their relationships. The writing contains the slang of the time and its style reveals each writer's social class. The entries also show enthusiasm fading over the years and a steady rise of other interests.

But despite the errors and lack of experience shown at the beginning of their venture into brewery matters, they built up a thriving business by sheer application and an appreciation of the essential tenets by which any business should be run. For capital, they had their portions from their families, but little after that; they had access to borrowed money, but had to pay the market interest rate for it. What they did have were contacts, which were vital in the search for free-trade business, particularly the military canteens and messes. They saw that the original heart of their business, the tied estates in York, was a falling market and that they had to look further afield to the industrial areas for both tied and free trade. They realized early on that good beer could not be brewed in York, and that quality was essential and had to be pursued relentlessly.

It may assist the reader if some brief biographical notes are given of the principal persons appearing in the pages of the diaries:

William Hotham

A member of an old established York mercantile family, which had owned the brewery and maltings in George Street since the early eighteenth century, together with a number of alehouses in the city. He was born in 1803 and it was his life's work to run the brewery, in which task he was joined by his nephew, Edward Hotham Newton. In 1875 they sold the brewery and maltings, with some 90 public houses in and around York, to a triumvirate for £36,000. The three gentlemen were Russell Henry Monro of Colton Lodge, York, Frederick William Browne of London and

Thomas Newton of Skelton Hall, near York. Why they sold is a matter for conjecture, but as Hotham was then in his seventy-third year and living in some comfort at the family residence of Fulford Hall, he had probably had enough of business. His nephew, then aged 45 and deeply involved in the civil administration of the North Riding, no doubt felt his time could be better disposed. Hotham died in his eighty-eighth year at Fulford Hall and was buried in Fulford churchyard, leaving the hall to his nephew. He is often mentioned by the partners in the pages of the diaries, and with some irritation when he called to collect his rents and the interest on his mortgage.

Edward Hotham Newton

The descendant of an old Knaresborough family and, as mentioned, the nephew of William Hotham and elder brother of Thomas Newton. He was born in 1830 and married three times. At the time of his first marriage he lived in Micklegate, York, then in a city residential street close to the brewery. After the sale of the brewery in 1875 he went to live in Scarborough, where he remained until the death of his uncle, when he moved to Fulford Hall. During his time at Scarborough he became deeply engaged in local administration, being a magistrate of all three Ridings, a deputy lieutenant of the East Riding and a member of the North Riding County Council. He was a director (and chairman) of the York City & County Banking Company, and also of the Yorkshire Insurance Company. He was well known for his generous and charitable stance. He died at Fulford in 1902 and was buried there. He left a widow, four sons and three daughters. He seldom appears in the diaries, but when he does it is mainly obscurely and in connection with the dispute between Thomas Newton and the then partners.

Russell Henry Monro

Little is known about this member of the triumvirate. At the time of the purchase he was living at Colton Lodge, York, but later moved to Clifton Lodge. In 1889 he sold his interest to Claud Lambton and his house to Reginald Parker, and departed for London and obscurity. Obviously a member of the upper county social circle, he was well heeled and vociferous in his views on men and matters. The early diaries are filled with the forthright statements he made regardless of creating hostility or favour. He threw himself into the practicalities of the brewery business and did not leave unpleasant duties to others to perform. He comes across in the pages as an engaging and infuriating man, replete with the self-confidence of his class but in no way depending on it. The diaries lost some of their human interest when he left. However, long after his departure his name continued to appear in the diaries in connection with various mortgages in which either he, his aunt or a professional firm in London carrying his surname appear – all ready sources of finance, the security being offered by the mortgage of public houses easily judged by him.

Frederick William Browne
Virtually nothing is known about him. He appears in relation to his partnership share taken in 1875, which he sold in 1884, and is mentioned in the entries about the dispute with Thomas Newton. One can only assume that he was a friend of Monro's and was invited by him to come in on a speculative venture.

Thomas Newton
A member of the Newton family and younger brother of E. H. Newton. There are no clues in the diaries about the quality of his relationships with his colleagues. After he sold his share to the other partners of the firm in 1885, he began a legal action against them on the grounds that he had received less than its value from them. However, he fell into such serious financial difficulties after the sale that he was prepared to abandon his action to seek their charity. He received some undefined help and was thereafter mentioned no more.

Sir Frederick Milner
Born in 1849, he was the second son of Sir William Mordaunt Edward Milner of Nun Appleton Hall near York, the city's representative in Parliament in the Liberal interest from 1848 to 1857. Having been educated at Eton and Oxford, in 1879, at a time when Hotham & Company needed funds to finance a

substantial property purchase from James Melrose, he and Reginald Parker took a share in the firm. From the beginning he took an active interest in the running of the business and this continued until it was turned into a limited company. In 1880 he married the daughter of the MP for East Retford, William Beckett-Denison of Meanwood Park near Leeds. In 1881, on the death of his elder brother who had reduced the family estate through extravagance, he succeeded to the baronetcy. In 1883 he became Conservative MP for York, which he represented until the 1885 dissolution. He returned to Parliament for Bassetlaw in 1890. On his election as an MP, Nun Appleton Hall was sold to meet the family debt and he went to live at Taplow Lodge, Maidenhead, Berkshire. He pressed for the welfare needs of discharged soldiers from the Boer War onwards and earned their gratitude. He died in 1931 and was buried at Acaster, near York.

Reginald Parker

Born in 1854, he was the sixth son of the sixth Earl of Macclesfield of Shirburn Castle in Oxfordshire. He was educated at Eton and thereafter spent seven years in banking, first at Child's in London and then at Lambton's Bank in Newcastle-upon-Tyne. While there, he came into contact with the family of the Earl of Durham, a large landholder in County Durham and the owner of the bank. In 1876 he married Katherine Ames, the daughter of another Tyneside banker who lived at Linden Hall near Morpeth in Northumberland; their union lasted 63 years. In 1879 he purchased a share in Hotham & Company and moved to York. From the start he took a leading role in the firm and for about ten years was closely involved in its day-to-day running. When it became a limited company he was its first chairman and he continued as such until a few months before his death in 1942. In all, he was connected with the brewery for over 60 years. However, he had a passion for horses, both racing and hunting, which involved him closely with the York racecourse and, to pursue this interest, he gradually began to leave the daily matters of the brewery to others, certainly from 1890. Then, in 1907 he sold Clifton Lodge, which he had bought from Monro, and went to live at Hurlingham in London. Both he and his wife found the

London scene – where he was a member of Boodles and the St James's clubs – congenial to their tastes and way of life. Nevertheless, he remained deeply involved in the brewery world and took on directorships of brewery companies in both the United Kingdom and USA. One of his three daughters wrote an account of her childhood and parents in which she unflatteringly portrayed her father as a remote, mean and egotistical man who cultivated people above him and ignored those below him.

James Melrose
He sold 50 of his public houses to Hotham & Company in 1879 and the transaction caused the partners, particularly Monro and Parker, much heartache and suspicious fury; they felt they had in some way been diddled and so treated Melrose with reserve.

The purchase took over a year to complete and the terms were so vague that he continued to supply his former tenants. Pages of the diaries are filled with the running disputes between them, recorded with baffled rage by the partners. Melrose was obviously too astute for the young men and, though not dishonest, he knew which gaps in the contract he could pass through with impunity. Also, he did not sell them his best houses and these drew trade from those he had sold to them; though he later sold these to them as well.

He was born in 1809, reputedly in Wheldrake, in a house opposite the village school he attended. He came to York and was articled to John Carr, a land surveyor in Stonegate. He then moved round the North of England carrying out surveys of estates for landed owners, but returned to the York area to set up a practice; he was particularly involved in surveying land required for railways, and in the preparation of plans and schedules for George Hudson, the York 'railway king'; he then went to the estate office of Lord Leconfield at Escrick in 1861. He left and became a partner with John Roper, a York wine and spirit merchant and, through him, took up his lifelong interest in horse racing.

Roper died in 1875, leaving Melrose sole proprietor and inheritor of the chairmanship of the York Racecourse Committee, in which capacity he inspired and oversaw considerable improvements to the course, its facilities and management. In more than

50 years' association with racing he was said to have only ever made one bet on a race, and that was the classic race in 1851 between Voltigeur and Flying Dutchman.

He served in public life and in office in the city for over 70 years as a council member, alderman, lord mayor, freeman, magistrate and public benefactor. He declared that throughout his life he had always followed the admonition of the Delphic Oracle – 'Nothing to excess'. He was the president of the Gimcrack Club and attended its annual dinner at the age of 100, bright in his faculties. He was a familiar figure in the streets of the city with his white carnation and red nose, so it was said. He had an old De Dion motorcar, his first and last, and when he was not using that he rode about in a brougham.

He died on 4 February 1929 at his home, Clifton Court, in his one hundredth year. He had an impressive funeral at the Minster, which 2500 people attended, and was buried in York cemetery, of which he had been a director. He left a brood of grieving children – six sons and one daughter. John J. Hunt, the owner of the Ebor Brewery, Aldwark, York, attended the funeral service, but none of his sparring partners of 50 years before from the early days of the Tadcaster Tower Brewery Company were there. Colonel Kirby, later to become a director, came as a representative of the racecourse committee. He was a man of meticulous habits who kept a diary throughout his life in which he recorded his daily doings and reflections. On New Year's Eve 1887, as the bells of the Minster rang out the old and rang in the new, he wrote: 'Arthur is at Glendive in Montana, America. John is in Berlin with his schoolmaster; Charlie, Jessie, Walter, Ernest and Harry are with us. I began life (business) on a salary of £50 per annum with Mr Carr in 1848, and I am now in receipt of £5000 per annum.'

The diary was in the possession of a wine and spirit firm in York with which he was associated, J. & G. Oldfield Ltd, which moved in the early 1960s into Melrose House, St Sampson's Square, York; they have vanished, which is a pity, as his diaries were a testament to provincial life and habits in the Victorian age.

The Lambtons

John George Lambton. Eldest son of the Earl of Durham of

Lambton Hall, County Durham and, with Parker and Milner, one of the trio who bought into Hotham & Company in 1879. No sooner had he found an occupation in life than his father died and, aged 24, he succeeded to the title. He took little part in the daily running of the firm, but provided a useful source of funds for it. In 1882 he married, though the marriage brought its own problems for him. He retained his share and became a sleeping partner.

Claud Lambton. Brother of John George who bought Monro's share in 1889. He lived at Grove Lodge in York and, with Parker and Dawnay, was very active in the business until he moved to London in 1907. He became a director on the incorporation of the firm in 1894 and continued as such until 1946.

Charles Lambton. Another brother who became a partner in 1891. He was a full-time career officer in the army and took no part in the business.

Francis Lambton. Also a brother who took a share in the firm in 1892. He was a trainer of racehorses.

Geoffrey Nicholas Dawnay
He purchased Lloyd's share in 1882 and became an active partner, continuing as a director after incorporation until 1907, when he resigned and was replaced by James Stephens, a partner in the firm of London accountants, Lescher, Stephens & Company, well known for over 60 years as auditors and accountants to the brewery trade. Dawnay was a younger son of Viscount Downe, of Wykeham Abbey near Scarborough.

Charles Howard Tripp
From Scarborough, but nothing is known about his early business career. The trio recruited him as general manager and he took up the position in 1887, thus giving them the freedom to pursue more enjoyable interests. He was very capable, instituting a system of regular financial appraisals on the progress of the business and the proper attendance to affairs of the firm. He lived at 11 Wenlock Terrace, Fulford Road, and at Holly Croft, York. He became a

city councillor, and the influence this gave him and his foreknowledge of events were of enormous assistance to the firm. He left Hotham & Company in 1894, just before it became a limited company, to become manager of Allsopp's Brewery at Burton-on-Trent. His tenure of office was one of considerable influence on the prosperity of the firm. He was very active in brewery trade matters generally and his judgement was sought and respected.

Cospatrick Thomas Dundas

He bought into the partnership in 1887 and took what might be described as a moderately active role in the business until 1894. He was brother of the Marquis of Zetland, of Aske, near Richmond, and had good contacts in the North to obtain the leases of public houses forming part of the landed estates of the region.

* * *

In passing, it is worth noting that, with the possible exception of Browne and Lloyd, all the other partners at some stage in their lives dwelt in Yorkshire, and moved in and belonged to the same social stratum of landed and titled gentry. They had much the same educational upbringing of Eton and Oxford and a family tradition in the hereditary ruling class; the Parkers, Dawnays, Lambtons and Milners were all interrelated in one way or another, and it was this structure that was a strength to them in their business dealings. Their families were large, and so long as the national economy was rooted in the land and what it produced, the patrimony was more than sufficient for their needs. The rise of industrialization altered these foundations of wealth and power to the disadvantage of the traditional landed families; younger sons were obliged to go out and earn a living from the portion of the estate advanced to them by their fathers. This was the position of Parker, Lambton and Dawnay, who brought to the task their inherited attitudes of authority, superiority and a refreshing refusal to accept at face value what was presented to them. This attitude may be compared with that of Melrose, a self-made man, in modern idiom 'streetwise', and with Tripp, much the same except that he was a forerunner of today's professional business manager, depending on his wits to earn a good living as a hired man and moving from employer to employer to achieve his goal.

There was still little difference between these two kinds, and business enterprise had not yet become so sophisticated that it required specialized training for both to flourish successfully; after 1919, however, the scene changed rapidly with the demise of the untrained but spirited amateur. Although he does not appear in the diaries, an example of this change is shown in Lieutenant Colonel William Lewis Clarke Kirby, a worthy local gentleman and member of the York Racecourse Committee, selected by Parker in 1941 as the man to lead the company forward. Parker was then 86 and Lambton 76; Kirby was 67, a retired regular artillery officer, magistrate and lover of country sports. The company meandered on under his limp guidance until it was swallowed up by a West Riding brewery predator. Kirby was a man of one era living in the next.

To understand the size of the market and its prosperity it might be useful to consider the social and economic position of York at the beginning of the 1870s, when the partners first began their diary. It is of ancient foundation and there is little doubt that it was a large and wealthy Roman centre that exercised power long after the Roman Empire collapsed. Just before the Norman Conquest it was reputed to be a city of 30,000 souls and busy as a Danish merchant centre. While one may question this figure, it certainly remained an important regional capital. Under the Normans it suffered for its loyalty to King Harold and declined; not until after the Middle Ages did it begin to recover, becoming the main city of the English kings in their struggle against the Scots. It declined again during the Wars of the Roses and only revived after the Civil War. At the beginning of the nineteenth century it was regarded as a dignified, northern capital with a population of 16,000. York's prosperity was based on agriculture and the wealth of the landed nobility around it, who turned to its skilled craftsmen to satisfy their needs and to its facilities and settled religion for physical and spiritual comfort. The country landowners had their town houses in York in the same way as those in the south had theirs in London.

The first catalyst for change was perhaps the coming of the

railway system in the middle of the nineteenth century. Itinerant workmen moved into the city to build the railway structures and, with the natives, began to form an industrial labouring class of significant proportions. The reliance on agriculture declined. The Irish flocked in, driven from their island by the famine and attracted by the hope of work. During the last quarter of the century other industries were established in York, mainly connected with cocoa products, but also farm-based activities such as milling, malting and brewing. By the 1870s the population had grown to about 50,000, and by the end of the century it was approaching 75,000, though exact figures are difficult to establish, particularly since the city extended its boundaries. The railways employed about 6000 men, the cocoa industry 3000 and the rest around 1000. So far as is known, wages were steady rather than exceptional; the city suffered along with the rest of the country in the times of economic depression, but not in the same way as the heavily industrialized cities dependent on one activity, such as cotton, coal, iron or wool. Nor were there prolonged labour disputes. A job could always be found, even if the pay was modest.

The partners quickly realized that they would not prosper if they depended on York to expand their brewery business; it was overstocked with alehouses left over from the past, in poor order, serving a drinking public with limited amounts of cash to spend. The partners all had experience of the busy industrial Northeast, with its engineering works, coal mines, shipbuilding, and iron and steel foundries; of the West Riding with its wool textile industry; of Sheffield and Rotherham; and of the east coast ports of Hull and Grimsby. In the York area the only hope of increased trade lay in the new military camp at Strensall. They vigorously set upon any new markets they saw, helped by the spread of the railway system out from the city both to travel and see for themselves and to send their beer quickly and in good condition. They even followed the flag abroad to the empire and sent their beer to India at a profit. Here Tripp, their manager, showed his worth; all new commercial ventures were costed to ascertain if there was any profit in the effort and, where possible within the United Kingdom, he went to see customers personally. These were novel concepts of business for the partners; they were prepared to visit in and around York, even a bit further afield, but persistently and regularly, not so.

The partners were astute in building their new brewery at Tadcaster – it enabled them to produce good beer, which could not be done in York. They saw the opportunities afforded by the railway system, but Tripp made real the spread of the business to the new thriving centres of working-class population. After he left in 1894, the company coasted along on the momentum that had been built up, but it slumbered through the twentieth century and was virtually the same at its demise in 1946 as it had been in 1900. Parker and Lambton grew old in the job and appointed as their successor a man in their own image – a familiar failing in closely controlled companies.

The problems associated with the consumption of alcohol are as old as English history itself. In the tenth century King Edgar tried to limit the number of drinking houses to one in each village, and the consumption by each customer. He failed; his limits instead became challenges to be exceeded. The government then changed its tactics and concentrated on quality. Ale conners were appointed to check ale at the brewing stage – a control exercised locally by town councils and justices who often added to their authority by decreeing who should be an alehouse keeper and when alehouses could open. With the continued growth in ale drinking, now hopped to become beer, the first licensing act was passed in 1552. This set out the basic principles current to this day – a licence from the justices to open a tippling house, which was renewable annually, plus any refinements the justices thought fit to add.

Drinking to excess became recognized as a problem that needed tackling during the reign of Elizabeth I; solutions were put forward regularly and without much success – it became the English bane. The puritanism of the Commonwealth period was followed by the laxity of the Restoration and drinking places multiplied; spirits such as gin, rum and brandy vied with beer and ale for the drinker's favour – coffee and tea were spurned and the coffee houses soon turned into better-class drinking holes. To keep out imports of cheap Dutch gin, in 1690 the government increased import duties and encouraged home-made spirits without control.

It was a disastrous policy, leading to Hogarth's pictured horrors of Gin Lane. All attempts to put the genie back into the bottle, as it were, failed, and gin shops were brought under the jurisdiction of the justices. By the end of the eighteenth century some control had been restored and the justices were ruthlessly suppressing unwanted licences. Also, social habits were changing: drunkenness in the upper classes ceased to be acceptable — George IV had died and Queen Victoria reigned.

The 1830s saw the rise of the temperance movement — a curious product of the urban growth that accompanied the rise of industrialization and the building of large housing estates. It drew its strength from these areas and, in established centres of population, its fervour replaced traditional allegiances between church and village. New accumulations of people (mainly factory labourers deprived of their familiar fabric of society) had no recreational pursuits other than the public house (and later the music hall), so they turned to alcoholic drink to escape from their everyday lives. The better off moved into their villas and looked down on the labouring classes in their wretched, rented dwellings in the ancient, decaying slums of the cities. The temperance movement grew quickly and ascribed all the misery of the lower classes to the consumption of drink — abolish drink and abolish drinking places, it was felt, and the problem would be solved. This battle raged throughout the nineteenth century. Bills advocating all manner of solutions were introduced in Parliament, but with the teetotallers becoming more and more extreme, any compromise capable of legislation became impossible. Public houses and beer houses, very old down-at-heel buildings in the slums, became the symbols of degradation and crime and, by association, were seen as their cause. For the rising lower middle classes, the path to respectability in society lay in the public assertion of abstinence and in the disapproval of licensed houses. Taking the pledge to abstain became a passport to respectability. A moderate attitude to drink and the patronage of public houses was unacceptable — a person had to be a teetotaller. Governments struggled to deal with this issue throughout the century, bit by bit introducing new laws against public houses and damning them as unfit places in which to be seen. Their function as traditional meeting places in which to conduct the affairs of local government was thereby removed. The Church severed its connections, then the magistrates, then the mutual benefit societies, until only the lower orders remained with the odious cause of their miseries. The off-licence shop grew in favour, with the virtuous sending out for their needs and consuming them in the comfort of their homes. The zealots wanted all public houses closed without compensation to their owners; when this failed they wanted local populations (by a majority vote) to be given the option of either closing down their public houses or limiting their hours of opening. The partners took large public meetings of the temperance movement and the counter-meetings set up by the brewers very seriously, for attendance at them, the clamour they generated and the strength of their resolutions were believed to influence government.

Participating in rallies for or against temperance was a kind of entertainment and a surrogate for religious belief. The government felt obliged, in common fairness, to suggest that if public houses were closed then hitherto lawful trading establishments were entitled to compensation, which simply provoked the teetotallers' demand for suppression to further extremes. During the First World War, however, the government brought in legislative action to assist the war effort by restricting the believed social harm of alcohol – opening hours for public houses were severely cut, the production of beer and spirits was controlled, prices were raised, measures were even instituted to prevent sale on credit, and the long pull and treating were introduced. By the time the war was over and the wartime measures revoked, five years had passed and drinking habits had irrevocably changed; the consumption of alcohol had fallen drastically. All that the teetotallers had campaigned for, other than the total abolition of the production of alcoholic drink and its retail outlets, had come to pass. The brewers realized that there was no future in dingy, back-street drinking holes – the war had raised expectations of better living conditions and leisure facilities. In pursuit of an 'Improved Public House' policy, the industry as a whole began to replace the prewar, men-only, sawdust-floor dives hidden in the back streets with large new licensed houses. It now wished to attract men and women, married and single, to surroundings of comfort, elegance and sobriety. There had been a sea change in people's habits. The teetotal movement had run its course and it petered out in the 1960s.

Public houses and older inns – where once coaches called and travellers slept and refreshed themselves – were badly hit by the coming of the railways. The new railway stations shifted the places to which travellers came and went, and new hotels and public houses grew up around them, leaving the old establishments to fade away. New public houses were built in the new residential areas, but only for the working classes. Having created the notion that respectability was synonymous with aversion to drink, the temperance movement had ensured that better-class residential areas built in Victorian towns and cities did not house any licensed premises, and this spread of public houses is apparent even today. These events are clearly reflected in the diaries and need to be understood in the context of the nineteenth century.

Nationally, as the notion of consistent quality gained ground with customers, public-house owners began to buy their beer from brewery firms rather than brew their own, and this trend gathered pace throughout the nineteenth century. It exercised the government from time to time as another aspect of the drink problem, particularly its concern about the quality of the beer being sold. In 1830 Parliament passed an act giving anyone the right to open a beer house without a justice's licence on the grounds that ale brewed by the owner on the premises would be better than that from a common brewer.

It was a law, like so many others, that came too late to correct the sin it was enacted to deal with, merely sowing the seeds of a further sin for correction in time. The big brewers could already see the market advantage of quality. Beer houses, like gin shops a century before, suddenly sprang up everywhere. The Reverend Sydney Smith, rector of Foston, a village near York, was moved to remark: 'The new beer bill has begun its operations. Everybody is drunk. Those who are not singing are sprawling. The sovereign people are in a beastly state.' Within a very few years almost all the beer-house keepers were buying their beer from the brewery firms and more beer than ever was being consumed. In 1848 an Association for the Suppression of Beer Houses was established; in

1869 a further act was passed making all houses that sold wine and beer obtain a justice's licence.

As mentioned above, this state of affairs led to the growth of the temperance movement, which had its heyday between the 1830s and the end of the century and caused much apprehension to brewers and licensees. The fervour generated among its adherents could be likened to modern-day movements such as Greenpeace, the Campaign for Nuclear Disarmament and other environmental protest groups, and like so many movements it weakened its cause by the excess of its protest. Governments considered the problem from time to time by appointing investigative committees and threatening dire action, but it was not until the Licensing Act of 1904 that justices regained absolute control over granting and renewing licences. In the process, existing licences, because they had been granted and because the justices were extremely reluctant to grant new ones, assumed a monetary value according to their geographical monopoly of the sale of alcohol. Attempts by the justices, within the limited powers granted to them by the 1869 Act, to cancel licences met with considerable opposition from owners, particularly brewery firms, and this opposition was only partially mollified by a statutory provision for the payment of compensation under legislation made in 1904.

The wheel had turned full circle by the middle of the twentieth century and licences once more were readily granted. Inebriation from alcoholic consumption has decreased, but has been replaced by a craving for other drugs, which cannot be regulated by tinkering with licensing laws. They require an organic change in people's attitudes. The sad and sordid isolation of drug taking will perhaps make people look back on the years of beer drinking and alehouses as the halcyon days.

Since the beginning of the nineteenth century it had been generally recognized that, apart from the extreme advocacy by the teetotal movement for complete renunciation of alcohol, there were other, more moderate solutions. The addiction to drink by the lower classes could, for example, be attributed to their abject conditions of life and housing, and improvements in these would, it was hoped, lead to a responsible attitude to their way of life. The spread of beer houses after 1830 overwhelmed this nascent idea with an avalanche of uncontrolled and disgusting drinking holes owned by people with no money to improve them. The government of the times was not yet attuned to the philosophy of state directed and financed public health measures. In fact, it was not until the middle of the century that the first acts to improve public water supplies, sewage disposal, control of health and the supervision of crowded residential areas were put on the statute book.

After the prolonged depression following the conclusion of the Napoleonic wars, the economy of the United Kingdom began to pick up and the lower classes found improvement in their lot and some spending money in their pockets. They were not content with squalid surroundings and hopeless lives; gradually prosperity came to them, and the public houses, with brewers' money, improved and left the beer houses behind. New ones were built, with large rooms, bright lights and an air of opulence and well-being. They had to do something to attract customers from the music halls and other places of public entertainment, for in the face of this competition beer houses and wine parlours had begun to decline during the latter part of the century. The various factions of the anti-drink movement, now fundamentally split over whether there should be total abstinence or just moderation, failed to notice the social changes going on around them. By the beginning of the twentieth century, big brewers with large tied estates in the industrial cities had not only become aware that it made good business sense to build new public houses with modern comforts in areas where the customers wanted them, but they were also removing public hostility to their commercial activities by demonstrably taking steps to put their own house in order. Whitbread in London and Butler in Birmingham were at the forefront of this move, which gathered momentum throughout the first half of the twentieth century. This, together with the municipal authorities' slum-clearance programmes, transformed licensed drinking houses.

The partners had bought into a brewery based in an ancient city already replete with alehouses and still heavily dependent on a local agricultural economy. Disraeli had just replaced Gladstone and the government's licensing bill, designed to tackle the drink industry, had been defeated in Parliament, though notice had been given that the legislators were not happy with the current state of affairs in the brewery industry. The farming community, particularly the corn growers, had been severely hit by the free-trade legislation and were to suffer many years of depression, culminating in a disastrous harvest in 1879. Industry in general was in recession and strikes abounded, with the London dock strike of 1889 being the most damaging. The miners had united nationally and brought power to the unskilled. Both the Gladstone and Disraeli ministries had brought in social legislation to reform education and the army, extend public health, improve working-class housing and revise local government organization. The old accepted order of things was collapsing around the ill-prepared partners. That they rallied and prospered is a tribute to their native adaptability.

Most of the public houses and beer houses the firm acquired in 1875 were situated in the poorest and most squalid parts of York – either side of Walmgate within the city walls – where courts and yards of tenement dwellings led off the narrow and confined main streets. Walking down the Shambles gives one some idea of what it must have been like, but one needs to bear in mind that then the streets were unpaved, there was no drainage other than a central channel, no water supply except common wells and no sewage disposal except middens with communal closets. The rows of wretched cottages were in an abysmal state of repair; their occupants were all tenants whose biggest weekly expenditure was the rent. Living and working were mixed up together, with all manner of trades, including numerous slaughter houses, jumbled in wherever they could be fitted. The stench was appalling, winter and summer. The most feckless of licensees ran the partners' public houses, striving to make a living where there was a licensed outlet for every 150 or so of the local population. The early diaries were filled with the troubles they had – with the tenants, the properties and the beer supplied. Their woes increased with the houses they bought from Melrose in 1879, a large number of which were in the same parts of the city.

Some of these houses were in better parts of the city. For example, new streets of cottages for the more affluent working class were being built in The Groves, Nunnery Lane and other artisan areas. But the difficulty from a beer trade point of view was that this class was less inclined to patronize public houses, preferring rather to send out for beer to the off-licence. Higher up the social scale, and well outside the city walls, residential areas did not want public houses at all. Clifton firmly declined such an amenity. In areas such as these there were just a few former country inns, which were swallowed up by the new houses going up around them in the expansion of the last three decades of the nineteenth century, and substantially that is the licensing position to this day. The partners did have a few of these outlets, which supported their best tenants. As previously mentioned, although they were unaware of the changes that were to come and overwhelm them, they knew they had to break away from their reliance on the old city slum areas and instinctively went along with the way the licensed trade was developing. The word 'instinctively' is used advisedly here; people caught up in a process of change are often unaware of it and, even if they are, rarely know which way to go. In hindsight it is easy to see what should have been done, but difficult at the time, particularly if this means persuading others to change course to suit one's intuitive leaning.

There are thousands of pages in the combined diaries, but after reading the entries for the first few months it quickly becomes apparent that they continually readdress the same problems, namely defaulting licensees, bad beer, indolent employees and falling down properties. Incidents were recorded haphazardly — those intended to read them were obviously assumed to have a background knowledge of them and an appreciation of the technicalities involved. To have picked out literal extracts from the diaries *tout court* would in many instances have been self-defeating, for few were followed through as complete stories.

Further, they require explanation for readers unversed in the jargon used or the customs and habits of the licensed trade. In the early days the partners' characters come through vividly and unselfconsciously in their writing styles — they use words and phrases drawn from their schooldays and domestic lives and these impressions are reinforced by the kinds of remedies they suggest for solving their various problems. Though the diaries lose their freshness and idiosyncrasy when Tripp takes on the task of keeping them, they nevertheless gain a certain continuity in that they enable one to trace the passage of events.

To extract the essence from the diaries – the establishment, management and development of a provincial brewery in the nineteenth century – and to make the story readily comprehensible to lay readers, I transcribed the significant entries and collated them into a sequence (they were often spaced far apart and not easily recognized as being the same event), translated their more esoteric parts and then fitted the events into the context of the partners' general activities. I have included entries that throw some light on their social and recreational lives away from the business, and from time to time enough statistics to show the firm's progress.

In 1875 the partners bought Hotham's brewery, maltings and offices in George Street, York, along with about 50 public houses in and around the city. Four years later, in 1879, they bought 50 more houses in the same area from James Melrose. Because the business was small and compact geographically, they ran it personally and directly from George Street without any intermediate managers. They themselves made the rounds of the houses, visited their tenants and witnessed their (usually) sordid businesses.

With the arrival of Milner, Parker and Lambton, the firm began to expand out of York and into the big northern centres of population. This meant they could no longer run it entirely on their own and so, though they continued to look after York themselves and to retain control over all decision making, they used upgraded clerks for general office administration and for inspecting houses, collecting rents and trade accounts, and evaluating new opportunities for expanding trade. Further afield, in places like Sunderland, Leeds, Wakefield and Darlington, agents were appointed to sell their beer and look for outlets, both for purchase and supply. The extensive rail network from York enabled them to go expeditiously to see and judge the work of their agents, and to send supplies to them. As trade built up, premises were acquired for use as depots and the change from agent to manager was effected; free public houses were bought to bolster the free trade by a tied presence; then all the agents were gradually replaced by free-trade travellers and tied trade inspectors.

By the time the firm was incorporated into a limited company in 1894, it had main offices and depots in Wakefield, Grimsby and Darlington, with smaller establishments in most of the big towns and cities, usually behind their best public house in the district.

In 1882 they built a new brewery at Tadcaster to cope with the increased business and, from its own siding, sent beer by rail throughout the North. With the appointment of Tripp as general manager in 1887, the partners gradually gave up all the daily administration, passing their time in other activities – hunting and racing, social life in London, holidays on the continent, and staying with relatives and friends in their country seats. Parker concerned himself with his other brewery company interests and Milner with his political career. They continued to use their wide contacts to bring in business for the brewery, principally for the handsome trade of the military camps.

The history of the survival of the diaries may be of interest to the reader. I first saw them in September 1946 when I visited the offices of the Tadcaster Tower Brewery Company Limited with the late Mr H. L. Bradfer-Lawrence, with whom I was staying as a house guest at Sharow, near Ripon. This in itself requires an explanation. My father and mother had died three years earlier, and because he had been a boyhood friend of my father's and had had a business relationship with him until his death, he took it upon himself to oversee my education until I could stand on my own feet, a care for which I shall always remain grateful. I was then aged 19 and waiting to go up to Cambridge University in the autumn of that year. He had asked me to stay, I think, in order to form an opinion of me, as elders in his position usually do.

At breakfast one morning he said he was going to York and asked if I would like to go with him, adding that he had just bought a brewery company there and had one or two matters to deal with. We went over to York and I clearly remember the car swinging off Piccadilly through some opened double iron gates into a cobbled yard with the offices we were to visit at the far end. The yard was filled with stacked empty casks and wooden crates. Motor wagons were being manoeuvred into position for loading against a raised platform and an almost visible tension was emanating from the men working there. Even as a young man I could detect the interest his arrival had created and the laboured effort they were putting into their work because of our appearance. A watchful silence spread across the yard as we walked to the office door; I could feel their eyes fix on us.

We went through the door and, once inside, were immediately met by a flustered man who had come out of a room on the left of the entrance, which had an inspection hatch opening out onto the corridor. He conducted us upstairs to a room containing a large table with chairs around it and a bookcase at the end. Everything was in shades of brown – the wallpaper, paint, linoleum and furniture – as if frozen in time in the 1920s. We stood in the room while the clerk went out again with the message that he would see if Mr— was ready. This displeased Mr Bradfer-Lawrence; his impatience was palpable and it made me feel uncomfortable. He looked up and down and moved his body with swift nervous little gestures, while I simply stood and waited. He then addressed me: 'Anthony!' he said, 'I shall not be long. Amuse yourself. See what is in that bookcase.' The clerk returned and he disappeared with him into the next room to meet two of the company's directors, whom I later found out were Colonel Kirby and Arthur Furniss. I could hear their voices through the walls; I opened the bookcase doors.

Among a line of dusty volumes, which so far as I remember were trade directories and magazines, was a set of leather-backed ledgers. I took one down and opened it on the table. It was handwritten and in the form of a diary. It interested me, for the first entry I read was a violent diatribe by an unknown person on the shortcomings of employees, with words underlined for emphasis, followed by similar entries in red ink, counter-statements in another hand, rebuttals and nothing more. It was frustrating not to know how it all ended. I read for an hour or so and then I heard the meeting next door coming to an end. There was a shuffling of chairs and then Mr Bradfer-Lawrence was standing in the doorway saying we were going; his hosts were hovering behind him in what appeared to me to be some apprehension. The parting words were brittle. I was introduced, we shook hands, went downstairs, got into the car and left.

Mr Bradfer-Lawrence asked me what I had done in his absence.

I told him I had read an interesting diary sort of book, and he replied, 'Oh yes, the partners' diaries. I saw them myself. What did you think of them?' Before I had time to reply, he had passed on to reading some documents he had with him, and we went silently all the way to Bradford and his brewery in Manchester Road.

The books with which I had amused myself were indeed the partners' diaries, which form the subject matter of this book, and the two men with whom I had shaken hands were Lieutenant-Colonel William Lewis Clarke Kirby, the company's chairman and senior director, and Arthur Furniss, also a director and the principal of a firm of solicitors he himself had established at Rotherham. Kirby lived in a village outside York, had a distinguished war record, was a devout churchman, served as a magistrate and concerned himself in county affairs. He was also a keen follower of the turf and it was through this contact that Parker asked him to become a director of the company. He was a man of forthright Christian virtues with a strong sense of doing his duty come what may. He was also somewhat eccentric in that he used the argot of military life and the hunting field in his duties in court and in public life generally, but he was a well-meaning man, albeit of limited vision. He died in 1962 at the age of 88.

Furniss was another kind of person altogether; he had been asked to join as a director before the war, on the death of James Stephens, of the well-known firm of brewery accountants, Lescher, Stephens & Company, of London. Stephens had been originally appointed a director to safeguard the interests of the debenture holders in the company, and Furniss was involved in brewery financial affairs through brewery companies in Sheffield and Rotherham, so it was considered he was a suitable person to have on the board. He liked to think of himself as an essential middleman in property acquisitions, taking his commission in the process, and he eventually fell out with Mr Bradfer-Lawrence on this – but this lay in the future.

There was another director whom I did not meet on this occasion, but got to know quite well some ten years later – Colonel Reginald (Squeak) Thompson, a racing crony of the others and the largest shareholder in a brewery in Bradford called William Whitaker & Son Ltd. He was an amiable man who was always in the company of his nephew, Christopher Thompson-Royds, his fellow director, and they were always squabbling. The nephew suffered badly from gout and wore carpet slippers much of the time; they were an odd but amusing couple on the Bradford scene of the 1940s and 1950s, floating between the gentlemen's bars of the Midland, Victoria and Alexandra hotels.

Their brewery used to be in the middle of Bradford, opposite the Alhambra Theatre, and in the 1920s they sold it as a site for one of the big new cinemas, which were then the rage; with the sale money they astutely built large public houses in the growing residential areas surrounding the West Riding cities, and even more astutely entered into an annual arrangement with Tetley, the big Leeds brewer, to supply the beer. To save themselves the chore of managing these enormously profitable houses, they let every one of them to tenants, who fell over themselves to get them; and lived very comfortably on the rents and the wine and spirit business, which they kept under their own control.

They ran this unusual empire from a plain small office and warehouse in College Road, off Manchester Road, Bradford, under the supervision of George Barrett, a long-serving and dour Yorkshireman. Squeak could devote his time to the study of racehorses and Christopher to drinking; it was a marvellous formula for success in the licensed trade, which fortuitously and felicitously they had chanced upon. It took until the 1990s, when the government authorized investigations into the drinks industry, for the light to dawn – owners of free houses had the brewers where they wanted them so far as getting good business terms were concerned; and further, if those owners wanted a quiet life, they let their houses on fair rents with a tie for beer supplies only, and made their profit out of the brewers' discounts. It was a situation with which the partners, 100 years before, were well familiar; greed, coupled with a statutory monopoly, gave the brewers a heyday from the beginning of the twentieth century until nearly the end of it. They could not restrain themselves and be cautious, and fell from their pedestal of good fortune.

All three resigned as directors and were replaced by the former general manager, A. B. C. Wilson, who had retired four years earlier, on the death of Parker.

Ten years had passed between my visit to York as a student and the next time I saw the partners' old office. In the meanwhile I had completed my education, lived abroad, returned to England and been invited north by Mr Bradfer-Lawrence, who was offering me the post of company secretary at his brewery in Bradford, then known as Hammonds' United Breweries Ltd. It had swept into its nest a considerable number of northern breweries, closed them, rationalized them and rearranged their properties. The partners' brewery at Tadcaster had been selected as the main supplier for a housing estate where the free trade far surpassed their wildest expectations. It had been enlarged and plans were underway for its imminent enlargement yet again. The wells and boreholes so laboriously dug, and so fractiously worried over, were not enough. Water was to be purchased from the Leeds Corporation water works; modern chemistry could alter its composition to make it just like Tadcaster water itself. The last of the railway sidings, once so important, were torn up to make room for motor wagons and their loading stages. The brewer's art and mystery were subsumed in technology; a good nose and a seeing eye were not necessary to brew good beer, but an ability to read dials and interpret what they said were.

I was made a director and secretary of the Tadcaster Tower Brewery Company. And, to give senior non-director members of Hammonds a sense of involvement, they too were made directors of Tadcaster Tower. I arranged monthly meetings in the partners' boardroom in George Street, where we sat round the table and signed documents, approved transfers of money to the parent company, considered the condition of the beer and were generally respectful to Mr Bradfer-Lawrence, who was the chairman and always in a hurry. Though the minutes I produced were even more opaque about what was decided than those written in the last diaries, the procedure of setting up these meetings, the assembly and the board luncheons at the Royal Station Hotel gave a certain sense of occasion and bestowed a warm feeling of position on those attending. Of course it did not last. Monthly meetings became quarterly meetings and finally annual meetings for the sake of legal requirement. Other matters pressed on the chairman's time and he ceased to attend; the warm glow of togetherness evaporated. Tadcaster Tower was wound up as a company some 70 years after it had come into being and vanished into history.

Hammonds too was swallowed up into a larger brewery, which needed a prestigious head office in the North of England – no less because it was called Northern Breweries of Great Britain Limited. Many of its directors and leading managers, now using the increasingly popular title of 'executives', were from the south, and to break them in gently to the rough northern clime, it was felt that York was a good halfway hôuse, particularly as the train service south was convenient and speedy. For the first time in the North, a brewery was being run by executives who saw no need to live 'on the patch', and whose commercial acumen, they were convinced, was of universal application in place, time and trade – a far cry from the partners' dictum that managers must live in their regions and be out and about in the trade day and night. Consultants from London advised on marketing, packaging, beer quality, incentive tenancy agreements and brewing beers at Tadcaster to match those of breweries that had been closed. All this fervent discussion took place, as a temporary measure, in the partners' confined and dismal boardroom; the executives were appalled at the little old-fashioned rooms they had to use for their spacious decision making. They picked up the atmosphere of the North and the rough and tumble of the trade in their frequent sorties to the Royal Station Hotel, and at weekends they returned to the south to ponder the action.

It could not go on like this, so it was decided to build a new office block. The old maltings on the site of the Maison Dieu of medieval charity were pulled down, as were the stables and empty cask store, and a fine six-storey building appeared in brutal exposed concrete and furnace brick, along with a penthouse suite and enough room to turn the chauffeur-driven limousines round for the Friday night departure south. The brewery trade was booming, with corporate change taking place so quickly that it took a strong vision to follow the action; no succeeding balance sheet and profit-and-loss account were like their predecessors; those involved had time – the next depression was still some 12 years ahead.

The company's new head office opened in 1962. Heals of London fitted out the penthouse and supplied the new office furniture, with the better items from the closed offices at Bradford brought in to furnish the top floor, which, like some inner sanctum of a religious institution, was reserved for the main board of directors – access to it was by invitation only. The George Street office boardroom table was moved to the penthouse dining room, and the Bradford boardroom table and chairs were moved to George Street; the family pictures from Lockwood Brewery, Huddersfield, hung on the walls – an unwonted unity unremarked by the new generation.

The George Street accommodation was turned into the regional manager's general office and I was given the job of clearing out 100 years of debris. We sent to the tip boxes of papers, ancient office furniture and any other bits and pieces that had no place in the bright new world we were building. I was determined to keep the diaries and a run of annual brewers' almanacs and yearbooks, for I was interested to read them as part of the brewery trade history. Since a large break-front bookcase in the new boardroom, brought over from Bradford, was empty, I thought it would be a good idea to fill some of the shelves as a stopgap measure and the diaries and almanacs served the purpose. Had I not done this, they would have gone to the tip.

The new head office served its purpose for barely a year; in 1963 another grouping of brewery companies saw the head office go down to London; York was left like an egg in aspic – clearly visible but with no obvious sign of support. The directors, the most senior executives and the consultants were at the heart of affairs once more. All they needed in York was a good office and a decent mess, with a comfortable bedroom or two for the occasional visit.

The offices were occupied by the regional company looking after the interests of the national group; the diaries gently gathered dust with the almanacs in the bookcase and remained there until 1984, by which time the national group had become international and keen incisive brains of senior directors were planning the future. York was geographically outside the true centre of the group's activities in the North, and all the services necessary to a large company were not under the same roof. So, a very big office complex was leased in Leeds and all the office services were brought into it. York closed and was sold; the remnants of staff were sent to occupy a closed public house in Walmgate, by now a respectable street in York. The George Street offices of the partners had been gutted and turned into a staff training centre, and the brown painted walls and the tiled floors swept away; now even the training centre was swept away and nothing remained from the past.

I took the diaries and the almanacs with me to the Leeds offices and put them into the strongroom there, with the title deeds, as a personal act of preservation. The move to Leeds had been carried out in accordance with the directives issued by the main board director responsible for the company's activities in the North. One of his working rules was that any buildings that were not retail outlets should always be smaller than planned requirements and, in any case, should discount any foreseeable extra space. He had several other homespun *idées fixes* – for example, toilets should be plain, utilitarian and uncomfortable, office windows should command a view unconducive to admiration and there is always room for at least one more body in an office beyond its design capacity. I felt it a minor triumph that I could find room for the diaries and almanacs; I had known them for so long and had always thought that their social and historical significance would be recognized one day.

This will perhaps not be through my literary efforts, but they might kindle interest in a historian yet to emerge.

THE DIARY

1

In the Beginning, 1879–1882

A day in September 1879

One of the new partners reported that he had seen Mr Weaver, the owner of a free public house in Goodramgate in York, who had informed him that his tenant, Beeby, had run away, and that he, Weaver, wanted to sell the property. Consideration of Mr Weaver's state of mind and his motives, or a thought on the part of the new partner as to the kind of business life he was about to embark on, were not revealed. On the same day the partners instructed Messrs Leeman & Wilkinson, solicitors of the city, to prepare the deed of partnership of the reconstituted firm of Hotham & Company, of George Street, York, in being since at least the beginning of the eighteenth century and, under the guidance of its new and youthful owners, about to enjoy over 60 years of substantial growth and prosperity.

13 October 1879

The partners recorded their dissatisfaction with the tenants of the public houses they had purchased from James Melrose, who saw no reason to observe their obligation to buy their liquor from the brewery. In fact, the suspicion was that Melrose was suborning his former tenants to continue to purchase their wines and spirits from his firm of Melrose & Roper. Perhaps the tenants felt no need to obey young men with little experience of the licensed trade; if so, they were due for a surprise. As the tenants were to find out over the ensuing years, with the partners' youth went energy and with their upper-class tradition went dominance. For the moment they decided to inform all Melrose's former tenants that unless they signed the partners' public-house tenancy agreement within the week, the notices to quit their public houses, given to them by Melrose when he sold out to Hotham & Company, would be enforced. It took a year for the sale to be completed, during which time it often formed the subject of irritated comment in the diaries.

15 October 1879

Mr Wright of Acomb attended in the office and the partner who saw him recorded that he was a 'very saucy fellow' and, perhaps worse, 'very independent'. He roundly declared that he was not one of Melrose's tenants and that Melrose could not transfer him or his business. It seemed that Mr Wright was a free-trade customer and that Melrose had sold the goodwill of supplying him to the partners – James Melrose was clearly a wily man. After some discussion, the partner stated that he would try to find Wright a free house, thus obfuscating the issue and preserving the status quo to give time for a satisfactory result to be worked out.

16 October 1879

Mr Booth of the Ship, York, came into the office to declare that he would rather leave than sign the new tenancy agreement, which would put him on a month's notice. What was more, he would set up a beer shop next door!

18 October 1879

Melrose himself came into the office and the partners confronted him about still trading with houses he had sold to them, despite having sold them both the right and the goodwill to supply these houses. Melrose apparently agreed that those were indeed the terms of sale, but there is no evidence of him agreeing to desist; one can only conclude that the discussion engendered more heat than light.

On the same day the partners took the opportunity to discuss their financial affairs and, in particular, their borrowing arrangements, as one of them was deputed to see Leeman & Wilkinson about Lady Wenlock's mortgage.

20 October 1879

It was noted that Jackson of the Grapes, in Tanner Row in York, was drinking and that his wife was generally away from home. This observation indicated, as did many others in the diaries, that the partners were getting round their properties personally rather than depending on reports from their employees. Their enthusiasm for their commercial venture ran high and they were inquisitive and perceptive in their investigations. Drunkenness was a real hazard until recent times and was prevalent not only among the licensees of public houses but in the licensed trade in general; many succumbed to the temptations of such a readily accessible supply. Also, in promoting wholesale and retail sales, it was considered good business practice to lead by example, i.e. by drinking the product. Today this threat has abated because of the general disapproval of excessive drinking, strict drink and driving laws, the high cost of alcohol, consideration of health risks and the rise in the popularity of alternative drugs with which to escape or create a sense of well-being.

21 October 1879

The partners agreed to let the Marcia public house in Bishopthorpe to William Hanforth and gave him permission to construct a bowling green in the orchard belonging to the house. Bowling greens were beginning to replace quoits and the other old outdoor amusements of tavern culture as attractions, not least because horticultural equipment had improved for cutting grass and making smooth lawns. Bowling clubs were established at public houses and throughout the summer months teams of players, taking on the name of the house, would play matches against other public-house teams on a home-and-away basis, thus ensuring business for the licensee who provided and bore the cost of maintaining the green. This practice continued until the 1960s when changing social habits and a sharp rise in the value of the land for other purposes brought about its rapid decline. Today few houses have such a facility; the sites are now used to accommodate customer car parks, steak bars, spaghetti diners or other foreign food outlets – often with the name of the house changed from the former George or Red Cow to titles comprising initials, allusions to transatlantic glamour or pretentious perversions of obsolete 'olde Englande' tavern names. Bowling greens with a good road frontage were often sold to provide petrol filling stations or housing estates and were lost to the brewery forever. Public-house cricket and football grounds suffered the same fate, for gradually they too ceased to function as centres for local activities. The attractions moved indoors and, with noisy machines designed to exploit the human desire for monetary gain, they became artificial, ephemeral and directed more exclusively towards the young. This has brought more youthful, less controlled customers into public houses and there is now little common ground for the mixing of ages or for the harmony and understanding which traditionally prevailed between a licensee and his clientele. Of course, all was not peace and contentment then as all is not chaos now, but the true substance and nature of the public house in the community has irretrievably gone.

4 November 1879

The partners had now had control of Melrose's 50 public houses for about two months and they took stock of their trading in them. It was recorded in the diaries that they been through the books and found that 'Melrose's tenants did 1546 for October, ours 2205, so it is our own houses [that are] letting us down; his are doing better than with him.' In other words, they were doing better business in the former Melrose houses than they were in their own, which meant that those houses were either better placed or had better tenants.

3 December 1879

This was a very trying day for the partners, who were perhaps trying to resolve all their problems before Christmas. Mrs Todd had applied to take the tenancy of the Phoenix, but on examination of her financial means it appeared she had not a penny of ready money. Mr Jones, the tenant of the Acorn, was given notice, but this was hardly surprising really, for he had not paid a penny off his trading and rent accounts since he took the tenancy. They discovered that Mrs Fowler (who was certainly a customer and most likely a tenant of a Melrose house) was using the partners' money to pay off her debts to Melrose. The Skip Bridge Inn, under a free-trade customer called Mr Wiley, was being sold up and the partners were losing their investment and their unpaid trading account. And finally, shortly before closing Mr Jones, who had received his notice earlier in the day and used up the time in between to get 'half drunk' (a percipient appraisal), came into the office. He was very excited about his notice to quit, so they cancelled it and gave him a second chance.

* * *

There are no other entries of any significance until after the Christmas holiday period, so presumably the partners went off for their two-day rest in a calm mood.

Incidentally, it is interesting to note how many references there were to free public houses being on offer for lease and in many instances from large estates in the county. Often named after their titled owner (Wenlock Arms, Worsley Arms, Leconfield Arms), their availability suggests that the trend towards brewery companies forming associations with tied estates, which took place rapidly in the last quarter of the nineteenth century, had already begun. Owners of large landed estates had come to realize that it was financially more advantageous to lease their village public houses to breweries than to individuals and, in the case of the partners, to people with whom they were already on equal social terms. By the early 1900s, most of the vacant houses had been leased and the system of tied houses was established for the next 80 years.

27 December 1879

The partners circulated a letter to their tenants stating that they had appointed Messrs Smith & Watson, of Pavement, York, as their agents for the sale of their bottled ales and stouts and that all tenants would be required to purchase their provisions from them. The letter was written from 'The Brewery, York', namely their

George Street premises from where they did their brewing, bottling and malting.

The George Street brewery extended from Walmgate through to Piccadilly. The brewing premises were at the Walmgate end, with the cask beer cellarage behind them, together with the wine and spirit stores and various storerooms. Converted terraced cottages facing onto George Street served as offices and a better quality house was situated in the yard leading onto Piccadilly. In the early nineteenth century a brick malting building had been erected in the yard alongside George Street, but it was demolished in 1960; the remnants of its wall still form the boundary with George Street and the malting embrasures are still clearly visible. When Piccadilly was widened, the main entrance to the brewery was moved from Walmgate; large double iron gates were set in the Piccadilly entrance and a cobbled yard led up to the office, with the maltings on its right; stables and storehouses, with access to the beer cellars through an arch, were situated on the left. Malting ceased at George Street towards the close of the century, but was continued at Clementhorpe, where the stables were also taken. In the 1960s the site was divided in half and an office block and car park built at the Piccadilly end; in the 1980s the remainder of the buildings were extensively altered to form modernized offices; the office building and former wine and spirit warehouse are all that remain of the original exterior.

All the houses they then owned were tenanted, for direct management had not yet become a consideration.

* * *

They began the new year as they had left the old by continuing to discuss with Melrose the value of the brewing plant being purchased and their concerns about still supplying the new tenants with wines and spirits. There were frequent references to drunken tenants, to the non-payment of rent and trading accounts, and to the issue of notices to quit because of these problems. The employees also presented more problems than usual — Hagley, a traveller for the firm, had incurred large trading debts because he had sold wines and spirits at excessive discounts and, in addition, the firm had not been paid. Discount pricing was clearly something that had not been resolved, for they had arguments in the diary about how it should be calculated. They also discussed the horses, a subject about which they felt they were on familiar ground, and came to the conclusion that they had two too many; they examined the dray horses' harnesses and felt that the halter straps were too tight and should be loosened.

27 January 1880

A partner wrote that he had seen someone from the Loan & Discount Company who had been most impudent. He had refused to accept 10.75 per cent interest and had demanded £4 in interest for a 27-day loan of £10, and that, according to this partner's arithmetic, was an interest rate of 1200 per cent! No further entry appeared to explain what this was all about.

14 February 1880

Mr Peacock of Darlington came into the offices and saw them about starting an agency there. He was offered 15 per cent off wholesale prices and seemed quite satisfied with the terms; he had agreed to write to them the following week.

23 February 1880

They saw Melrose again about the price he wanted for the brewing plant, which was lying in a warehouse Melrose wished to clear for letting.

On the same day they also saw Mr Whitwell at the Excise Office, and learned they would have to pay excise duty and get a contribution from Melrose; if not, they would have to produce their account and brewing books, and appeal. It was yet another matter to be taken up with Melrose with no great expectation of success.

Brogden, a brewer from Leeds, was reported to be buying up all the free houses he could lay his hands on – as indeed, were the rest of them.

February was a time for reflection on the proper running of the business; a partner wrote into the diary the following rules to be followed by anyone visiting their houses:

1. To ask to see the cellar and the beers and report on the condition of both.
2. To report on the cleanliness of the house, utensils and glasses.
3. To ascertain what casks are in the houses and to see that empty casks and jugs are returned.
4. To watch carefully to see if a house is trying to set up a deal for spirits elsewhere.
5. To visit every town house once every week, every country house once every month and enter written reports in the book and show partners such reports.

It is unclear whether these sensible rules were written for the observance of partners and employees alike, for just one or other of these categories, or were merely an outburst of diffused enthusiasm. But it was clear, and always had been, that, like the Ten Commandments, they were absolute truths, but prone to human failing. Rule 5, one suspects, was more often breached than honoured because of the sheer logistics of the exercise. But at least they understood the essentials.

28 February 1880

The justification for Rule 3 quickly became apparent — they complained among themselves that they had only 1500 of Melrose's casks, whereas there should have been nearly 3000; too many customers were keeping empty casks and not returning them to the brewery. They discussed Melrose's brewing plant again and decided to have it removed from the brewery premises. The only problem was that they did not think they would be able to find anybody to do the job at a fixed rate.

2 March 1880

Two of the brewery's outside inspectors, Thorburn and Laxton, reported having discovered other brewers' beers in a number of their public houses. The culprits supplying this contraband beer were Tom Smith & Sons, of Leeds.

On the same day the partners talked about the brewing plant they had purchased from Melrose, but which they were unable to remove because it was embedded in the structure of his brewery buildings. They considered trying to sell it back to him, but being aware of their predicament the offer he had made them was derisory. One of them was deputed to see Melrose again in an attempt to get him to raise his offer.

Messrs Leeman & Wilkinson, their solicitors, were pressing them to finalize the purchase and mortgage of the 50 houses they had bought from Melrose the previous autumn; they fixed on the first Thursday after 6 March as completion day.

13 March 1880

An interesting entry in the diary read 'Send George Hudson notice of mortgage'. Could this be a hitherto unrevealed addition to the railway king's tangled financial affairs and a diversion out of railway stocks into brewing? No, he had died in 1871 and is therefore absolved. It appeared to be a modest free-trade loan to a namesake; a later entry stated that he would pay £80 by Friday next and the balance of £250 by 1 August.

15 March 1880

Thorburn's sleuthing was paying dividends, though bringing unwelcome news. He reported that no less than five tenants were purchasing spirits illegally from Melrose. Thorburn was then set to watch their houses by night, and for the time being nothing was to be said. This perennial problem in relations between brewer and tenant resulted from the tied house system and the guaranteed livelihood it brought. The brewer would let his public house at a low rent and make his profit by forcing the tenants to buy their supplies from him at higher prices than those charged by unscrupulous wholesalers who had been freed of the burden of maintaining public houses. The tenants in return, had practical, if not legal, security of tenure, without having to worry about administration or property repairs, so long as they sold plenty of beer and paid for it. They sacrificed their livers and their independence for a secure living. The problem the partners were facing with their tenants was that of discipline and they were forced early in their business venture to look carefully at their procedures.

Tied beer evolved from the brewer's need to sell his product, which had a short life, to an established market so that he could turn his attentions to large-scale production. It was a mercantile system of considerable antiquity, like grinding corn, both of which turned into monopolies. Nevertheless, there were advantages for all concerned so long as no single party gained an overwhelming or oppressive economic advantage over the other. The partners were short of cash and heavily indebted – over £60,000 would have to be found later in the year to pay Melrose for his houses. No wonder they agonized over accounts and running the brewery.

17 March 1880

Frederick Milner, who had been admitted as a partner in August 1879 and was anxious about getting married, inheriting his family's financially depleted estate at Nun Appleton and whatever else the brewery expected of him, announced that he was going to Cairo to get away from his problems for a while – a diversion made possible by the opening of the Suez Canal ten years earlier and the excellent travel arrangements provided by the Peninsular and Orient shipping companies, whose steamers plied the east–west routes. The other partners would see him again when he returned – sometime.

27 March 1880

The remaining partners wrestled with the daily problems. They discussed Richard Tetly (*sic*), tenant of the Cricketer's Arms and thought his rent of £15 a year for such a good house was absurdly low. He was given notice to quit. On the face of it, it was a hasty decision without negotiation, but perhaps there was more to the matter than had been recorded.

8 April 1880

They reviewed the office system for collecting money and found it wanting. Mr James, the solicitor, was felt not to be collecting in the debts as energetically as he might.

They noted that there was little advantage in keeping copies of letters dispatched without recording the names and addresses of their recipients on them. Furthermore, a good impression could not be achieved unless the writer used the copying ink specially provided by the firm for the purpose.

Regularly they sent to two of the non-active partners, Frederick William Browne, of Devonshire Place, London, and Thomas Newton, of Skelton Hall, their drawings of £62 10s a quarter – a small return at some 2 per cent on their £12,000 investment, it might be thought.

Later in the month one of them delivered a written homily about the state of the *Cask Book*, in which all movements of casks were supposed to be recorded; not mincing his words, he said it was a perfect farce, there were hundreds of casks missing and unaccounted for – probably, he gloomily suggested, having been broken up or sold by the tenants.

It was a constant problem for any brewery or returnable container business; a cask was an expensive item, easily disposed of for cash and almost impossible to trace. The problem still exists, even with sophisticated modern methods of keeping records, for aluminium casks can easily be melted down into ingots in backstreet smelting furnaces and obliterated forever.

They castigated themselves in April; they had been far too lax about serving their tenants with notices to quit. Verbal dismissals were given, but later nobody knew what had been done and confusion resulted. An order was given that all notices had to be in writing.

They prepared a list of tenants who were doing no business because they were either too old, too useless, too idle or drank too much. They would have to be weeded out by degrees.

Inserted at the back of the 1880 diary is a list of the houses acquired from Melrose; all were in or around York – the furthest from the city being at Easingwold.

There was a further note about the brewery plant they had bought from Melrose and were trying to get rid of. In the end they sold it piecemeal and hoped to clear £250, which seemed to satisfy them.

They parted company with Thorburn (no reason was given) despite his apparent sleuthing abilities, promising to help him if he got a pub of his own in Newcastle-upon-Tyne – a case of the gamekeeper turning poacher. They also got rid of their traveller, Hagley, for they could not tolerate the debts that always accompanied the trade he found. The parting was obviously amicable, for he received a quarter's salary as compensation. From the way numerous entries on selling in the free trade were phrased, one gains the impression that they disliked this side of the business – it was almost more trouble than it was worth. Also, it was not thought of as the gentlemanly side of the brewing business. Selling, which the brewery's roughnecks were made to do on sufferance, exposed the 'trade' side of the business, with its disguised price cuts, bargaining, bad debts and lack of respect from customers, whom they realized might sell their beer more cheaply than in the tied houses – which of course they did in the working men's clubs. Had the brewers been more astute and less snobbish, the clubs' brewery cooperatives would never have become established in the industrial conurbations.

22 May 1880

George Hudson and his debt resurfaced. He was obviously a free-house owner to whom they had lent money, for the partners promised that if he paid the balance by 1 August they would not foreclose on the mortgage.

Thomas Newton wrote in the diary that he was going abroad, and left his address as Poste Restante, Aix les Bains.

The partners felt it was time they laid down some more rules for themselves, so pursued a kind of teach-yourself management course for brewery executives. They wrote into the diary a set of questions they would ask prospective tenants:

1. Married or single.
2. How many children. [One does not know if this question in any way depended on the answer to the first.]
3. Been in publican's business before.
4. Do they mean to engage in business as well.

The last question is interesting. Apart from very busy pubs in the centres of large towns and cities, it was traditional for the publican's wife to look after the pub during the day and for the husband to take over in the evenings when he had finished working at his principal job (usually in farming, carting or a trade). Tenants who relied solely on a pub to earn a living were in the minority. It is therefore interesting (and a reflection of the firm's tied estate) that the brewery's pubs were thought to have been successful enough to support a tenant exclusively.

The partners then set out a list of what prospective tenants needed to be told:

1. The valuation [i.e. the furnishings and stock in the pub] must be paid down or a balance secured safely. In other words, penniless hopefuls need not apply.
2. One month's agreement. Tenants were on a monthly tenancy; they could hardly put down roots or invest money in the business on this kind of security. But the reality was different – a good tenant had nothing to fear, for the brewery was only too anxious to keep him and, being a good tenant, he did not want to be tied to a longer notice, for it stopped him moving swiftly to a better house.
3. Valuations were to be protected, i.e. returned when the tenant left. This meant that any furnishings purchased when the tenant entered the pub had to be left behind on departure for the incoming tenant; otherwise there was a theoretical danger of the premises being left empty; theoretical, because the contents of a house were worth more as an entity in that house than ever they were singly.
4. Accounts to be paid monthly and settled before the next delivery. This was a sound rule in theory, but it often fell down in practice because if the tenant could not pay for his beer and did not get further supplies the pub would either have to close because there was nothing to sell or the defaulting tenant would turn to a pirate supplier and thereby break his tie with the brewery, which lost all ways. Still, it was a useful guideline and an indication of the haphazard nature of commercial practices of the time.

This led the partners to consider the whole question of carrying out valuations of the pub's furnishings when the tenant changed. They thought the system was monstrous and ought to be stopped – it was robbery on a grand scale. They noted that Jackson, the tenant of the Grapes (Tanner Row, York) had paid £60 when he went into the tenancy of the house, but now that he was leaving was demanding £200 for the same collection of furnishings.

What really enraged the partners was the bypassing of an embargo on payment for goodwill by incoming tenants through the device of inflating the value of the furnishings. Breweries refused to countenance the existence of goodwill as one of the public house's assets on the basis, quite rightly, that the trade a house might do resided principally in the personality and business acumen of the current licensee, and not in the location or attraction of the house itself — if a successful tenant left he would either take his following with him or it would simply evaporate, in which case good money could not be paid for a will o' the wisp. Outgoing tenants saw the situation differently; in their view, they had spent a number of years building up a good business and were not prepared to pass it over to the incoming tenant for nothing — even though, on coming into the tenancy, they themselves had paid nothing for the then existing trade. Since brewers took little interest in what outgoing tenants charged for furnishings, or how these were valued, prices were picked out of the air and depended on what the tenant thought he could command from an inexperienced incomer. If trade had dropped during his tenancy, he would try to recoup his losses on leaving by demanding more for furnishings than he himself had paid. This happened often enough for valuation figures to get wildly out of step with the real value of second-hand bar furniture.

By the end of the nineteenth century the larger brewery companies in England had brought the matter under control by insisting that both outgoing and incoming tenants use qualified valuers, who laid down rules about what could fairly be included in an inventory and provided a basis for the valuation. I myself had some experience of such a situation when I took over the administration of a brewery on the Isle of Man, where the system still operated in much the same way as it had done during the time of the partners, and I could appreciate their indignation. Outgoing tenants were demanding prices for their furnishings that were often four or five times their actual value, and this effectively prevented houses changing hands. The brewery itself was then forced to take over the tenancy, settling at a figure by haggling, place the house under direct management, improve the quality of the furnishings and trade, and then put the house back onto the letting market. The cost had to be carried by the brewery and written off.

To their credit, the partners saw the problem and dealt with it. They started by stating that if the brewery had to take over a house, they would employ a reputable valuer, Tom Wright, who would make the valuation on a fixed basis and ignore the question of goodwill. They also decided that neither the brewery nor any outgoing tenant would be allowed to employ Roe as a valuer. And finally, no outgoing tenant would receive more than he had paid on becoming a tenant. Undoubtedly the word got around the trade, and though the rules were undoubtedly stretched to deal with difficult cases, the new order gradually prevailed.

27 May 1880

The partners saw Melrose about illegally supplying their tenants with spirits. However, he would only go so far as admitting that he might have 'sent out a few gallons of rum' to a tenant and 'breathtakingly' assured them that it would never happen again!

On the same day, soon after their heroic stand on tenants' valuations and venal valuers, they came to the conclusion that Tom Wright was not as good as they had thought; in fact he was as bad as Roe. There was no salvation for them anywhere.

17 June 1880

They looked at their stable expenses and worked out that each horse cost them 24 shillings a week, which was what a livery would charge them.

They worried about General Willis and wondered whether he would pay them their rent for the stables they had let to him. If the army depressed them, the cloth surprised them — Reverend W. Lawrence paid his account of £15. It was worth noting in the diary.

General Willis had been a hero in the Crimean War and Egyptian campaign; now he was commander of the Northern Military District and based in York with his horses. The stables were probably behind the brewery's Light Horseman pub, near the barracks.

7 July 1880

Russell Henry Monro, one of the partners who joined in 1875, lived at Colton Lodge and supplied the brewery with hay from his estate there. It came to the attention of the other partners that the hay had been wrongly weighed, and they were receiving four hundredweight less than they had paid for; it was not recorded how this was handled between them.

16 July 1880

There was a note in the diary to the effect that 'there was not a cask of Double X in the place, and not enough Treble X for business'. This entry was then crossed out in pencil and a hand had written 'a mistake'.

21 July 1880

General Willis sent his aide-de-camp round to the office to pay his rent. Monro was in and took the opportunity to enquire about supplying the military canteens with beer at the forthcoming manoeuvres. Their anxiety was such that Monro lost the rent cheque, so on the ...

24 July 1880

Monro was sent to the general's quarters to admit the loss. While there, he raised the matter of the beer supply with the general, who suggested he saw the canteen officer of the militia. As reported, it involved supplying beer at Aldershot. Monro persisted in his quest and found out that the canteen officer was Captain Reed of the Infantry Brigade.

The question of Lady Wenlock's mortgage had arisen again and they went to see Leeman & Wilkinson. They were concerned about their attempt to get the money they had spent on improving the mortgaged houses taken into account when considering the value of the security. This was a constant problem when several properties were being mortgaged to secure a loan; the mortgagor would endeavour to withdraw one or more of the properties from the security after some years to provide security elsewhere for a separate loan, arguing that because of capital improvements the remaining properties provided an equivalent security.

5 August 1880

They considered the state of their houses, prompted by a warning from either the licensing justices or the county health officer that the privy at the Angel, Easingwold, was still not improved despite promises that it would be attended to; a summons would be issued unless it was repaired at once. This led them to don the collective hairshirt and note down the state of repair of their estate, most of which had leaking roofs, blocked drains and no paint on the walls inside or out. They were prepared to offer the tenants free materials if they would undertake to do the decorations themselves. The offer was frequently taken up, though whether the work was ever done or if so how well and with what colour schemes, was never really established. The tenants' own decorations over the years tended to reveal strange colour combinations and a certain crudity of execution. The partners entered the brewing trade just as central government was beginning to pass public health legislation. A few years earlier nobody would have shown any interest whatsoever in the state of public-house toilet facilities.

13 August 1880

Some good news – Mawer, the traveller, reported that a new outlet would take the brewery's beer at a 15 per cent discount, despite better discounts from other Tadcaster breweries.

On the same day there was an entry that they had telegraphed Reed & Company, the London brewers, for 50 kilderkins of stout, which would indicate that they needed it for a special order – perhaps something to do with the militia – or that there were problems about the quality of their own beer. On the following day they went to Leeds to see if Tetleys would let them have 20 hogsheads of stout at 20 per cent discount for cash on delivery; but Tetley's could not deliver before the following Tuesday. On 16 August Reeds sent through 25 kilderkins at 10 per cent discount, and Tetley's sent 30 kilderkins at 22 per cent discount.

24 August 1880

Disaster struck! The copper coil of the boiling pan in the brewery burst; they patched it to keep it going and ordered a new one, and the following day they saw Mr Tangye's agent and ordered a 7 x 4 special steam pump, which would work down to 20 lbs pressure per square inch. They liked recording their appreciation of technical data and went on to explain to one another in several hands what the technicalities involved, and that gun metal should be used as a lining to the pump because of the corrosive nature of the water used in the brewery.

25 August 1880

Mr Gladstone, in his second administration and well on the way to becoming an old man in a hurry, was looking at the revenue-raising instruments of the state and, in particular, at excise duty. He felt that public-house owners offered some scope, for they benefited from a monopoly and could well afford to pay more for the privilege. He therefore introduced into Parliament a bill that would require an excise licence, in addition to a justice's licence, to sell liquor from the premises. Each public house would have to obtain a licence from HM Customs & Excise and pay an annual fee in duty based on the rent of the house — the higher the rent, the greater the duty. The whole brewery trade, including the partners, were in an uproar. If this were permitted, they reasoned, house rents would fall because the tenants, who would have to pay the duty, would deduct it from their rents. Ultimately, the law was passed and lasted until 1967. An annual value was ascribed to all licensed houses and duty levied at varying levels, depending on the chancellor's financial exigencies. It was an easy and cheap tax to collect and the brewers were unable effectively to oppose it.

31 August 1880

Biscombe, the brewery's building surveyor, reported to them that he knew of a fine artesian well at Clifton Asylum with good water; he thought it might be useful for brewing. They obtained a sample and had it analysed. They were beginning to realize that brewing in York would have to cease if their beer was to have a reputation for quality.

They noted on the same day that 17 September was fixed for the final completion of the purchase from Melrose and that he would affix his signature to their mortgage to him. Originally this matter was to have been completed the previous March; perhaps Melrose felt justified in persisting to sell to his former outlets irrespective of the terms of the contract so long as his sale money remained outstanding. The partners worried about how much the beer trade they had bought would cost them.

7 September 1880

General Willis sent a cheque for £15 round to the office to replace the one Monro had lost; they sent back an indemnity.

9 September 1880

The partners were still thinking about the quality of their brewing water; they took soundings and were informed that Cartmell, of Burton-on-Trent, was the best man to consult on the matter.

13 September 1880

Monro spent five hours at the barracks and came back sanguine that they had got the canteen supplies, so long as they produced 'good stuff'. Monro had ascertained that the canteen consumed 12 hogsheads of X every four days, three hogsheads of Treble X and two hogsheads of porter. Payne, the brewer, was told to send Double X marked as X, and as it was drunk in four days, he was not to put in any bisulphate of lime. The purpose of the first deceit was to impress the canteen – Double X was stronger, so the drinker would think to himself 'If this is just their ordinary mild beer, what must the Double X be like?' – tortuous thinking. The bisulphate was added as a preservative and corrective to the brewing water.

14 September 1880

Events had a tendency to arise to justify the partners' fears. It was reported that five casks of X ale had gone sour; they blamed the water. They also discovered that quite a lot of beer was being given away to tenants as an established custom when feasts were held in their houses for clubs, societies and the like, particularly involving cabmen. They did not like this one little bit and suspected it was prone to abuse. They stopped it immediately. Needless to say, this caused great resentment.

15 September 1880

They received an order for the military canteen with a message that the canteen sergeant would call the following day concerning polo. After their meeting with him they wrote in the diary that they could not supply X quality ale at the price quoted by the sergeant. They gave him £5 for his trouble. Perhaps their exploit of 13 September was backfiring on them?

18 September 1880

A day later than set down they went to the office of Mr Cobb, Melrose's solicitor, and completed the purchase.

21 September 1880

The Military Canteen Committee had let it be known that it was well satisfied with the beer so far supplied.

27 September 1880

The brewer reported that he thought the X beer for the barracks should be marked AK and not AX; the partners had no objection. This was curious because it turned beer from mild to ale, selling at the same price.

28 September 1880

The police gave word that, despite two previous cautions, Leaper, the tenant of the Grapes, of King Street, York, was still harbouring prostitutes and his licence would be in jeopardy at the next Brewster Sessions the following February.

18 October 1880

The partners discovered that the brewery had been left unattended, for Hartley was away ill and Payne had not returned that morning as arranged. They sent him a telegram 'BE GOOD ENOUGH TO RETURN AT ONCE. WE EXPECTED YOU THIS MORNING.'

26 October 1880

It was barley-buying time. They declined delivery from Mr Daniels because it was not up to sample: 'Why not buy barley we can brew with?' is firmly written in the diary. They felt Yorkshire barley would lose them the chance of doing any free trade in the next year. They bought Danish barley instead — 400 quarters.

6 November 1880

Monro saw Payne, the brewer, and paid him £50, making his salary £250 for the year to 30 September last. He was allowed to keep the whole salary of any pupil he instructed; presumably, the partners allowed him to charge a fee and retain the sum.

17 November 1880

They learned that the Barrack Tavern might be required by the government as a site for artillery barracks.

A fierce complaint appeared in the diary about the gross carelessness and neglect of the cooper in allowing 13 casks to leak 'fearfully'. A pencilled note next to the entry said it amounted to only two gallons in all.

24 November 1880

A joint note appeared about whether they could distrain for a particular debt due to them; they all wrote in what their legal friends had advised them — the advice differed widely.

23 December 1880

The military canteen returned two casks of bitter, saying they were 'quite hard'. The partners observed 'they were long-suffering, but that the partners would outstay them at last' — whatever that might have meant.

5 January 1881

They complain about the barley Monro had bought from Shaw being 'simply filthy, and could not be sold in the market for more than 30 shillings per quarter, whereas it was bought for 36 shillings'. They finally settled up with Shaw at 32 shillings.

28 January 1881

They were concerned about an employee, L. Smith, who had been ill for a long time and was unfit for work; they felt something would have to be settled about him.

4 February 1881

The partners found themselves in a mess because the office rules had not been followed in setting up a tenancy; a worthless fellow called Cooper had been given the tenancy of a house and let into possession without signing any document at all, without paying for the ingoing valuation of the furnishings or without even signing a bill of sale in respect of them. It turned out that he had no money and was known to be 'a bad one'. This sparked off a series of entries in the diary by the partners, the righteous ones insisting that proper investigation of any prospective tenant's finances was essential, that he must pay for the valuation before entry and, if he could not, then he either took the tenancy as a furnished house or gave a bill of sale. This progressed to a search for the person responsible for the letting, and then the discovery that Cooper had not yet even signed his tenancy agreement for the Bay Horse, six days after the enquiry had begun. The partners had truly fallen out among themselves, for one of them wrote in pencil, 'it would be more to the point if a certain partner instead of writing the words "should" and "must" so much, would substitute "has been" with regard to the furious attention to tenants' – an obvious reminder that past action was preferable to insufferable moralizing from chair-bound colleagues. It was noted that Acton, the traveller, had been sent to see Cooper, who was not in, so would be seen again the following day. Then followed a series of entries recording agreements and bills of sale, which had been signed, and the storm subsided – well, nearly.

12 February 1881

A note that Cooper must give a bill of sale by Monday without fail; the original investigating partner had discovered that a bill of sale had not yet been given.

16 February 1881

Henry Lloyd, the partner who lived at Scarborough, telegraphed the Woolwich 16th Lancers that Payne, the brewer, would call the following morning. Payne was put on the train that night. Apparently, important potential customers warranted the attendance of the brewer himself upon them.

The squabble of 4 February had not completely died down, for it turned out that the tenant of the Penny Tap, Bishop Auckland, had been in occupation for some considerable time and had not signed any agreement or paid any rent. He was sent for and came to York on the 19th and signed up.

21 February 1881

Brett, the traveller, reported he had obtained a large order from the 5th Lancers' canteen. This was balanced by the news that Payne's visit to Woolwich had been a disaster; the canteen sergeant stated that he had never been as shabbily treated as he had been by Payne and that he wanted £10 for his trouble.

It was noted that the old horse, Boxer, was ill and that the veterinary surgeon had considered it necessary to move him as he was suffering from the strangles, an infectious throat disease.

23 February 1881

The partners again considered the application for a tenancy by Lord Wenlock's coachman. They offered him the Saddle, Fulford. The ingoing valuation was not worth more than £200, they thought, but the outgoing tenant, Leafe, was holding out for £327 – what he paid when he went in. The partners felt it was all humbug.

On the same day Reginald Parker wrote in the diary an offer to the others of the use of his quarter cask of private sherry in the cellar, and he would order another lot. He said there was just sufficient Number 1 sherry left to supply Brook House.

28 February 1881

It was agreed to instruct the solicitors to prepare a power of attorney to permit any three partners to sign documents on behalf of the firm. Until then, all had to do so, which made business matters difficult, at least when one of them was abroad or away from the office. One must assume that this was why they entered their holiday addresses in the diary.

16 March 1881

Fender, bandmaster of the Yorkshire Hussars, wanted the tenancy of the Robin Hood, but could only find £50 for the ingoing; one partner wrote 'No' with an exclamation mark, and another, in pencil, 'Bad Hat', in the slang of the times. Fender was not appreciated.

19 March 1881

It was noted that 15 cases of champagne had arrived from 'Peignons', along with an acid remark that the only consumer was Mrs Newton of Scarborough, who very occasionally took two dozen, the last time being in 1879. The same partner mentioned that they already had 11 cases of better champagne in stock. Seemingly, someone was getting at someone else's relative.

21 March 1881

Monro had been through the outstanding accounts, and entered in the diary a list of those which 'must be attended to'; Monro had a way of raising matters and hackles at the same time.

31 March 1881

A familiar complaint arose; the waterworks company 'must be seen to' (another Monro investigation without doubt). The company had doubled the charges for water, for a consumption of 600,000 gallons per quarter and the brewery used hardly any! He suggested the meter should be checked. Few things really change in the business world!

1 April 1881

Not an All Fools' Day joke; the drain at the Ship, King's Staith, York, was stopped up, apparently due to the waste coming from the adjoining building's pipes. The partners had doubts about doing anything to resolve the problem until the urban sanitary authority had been consulted. History does not record what happened in the interim.

5 April 1881

They received an insurance premium demand from the Yorkshire Insurance Company, due on the past Lady Day. Nobody knew anything about the policy; the entry is crossed 'Where is it?'

16 April 1881

The water bill is discussed again; water costs are £120 a year – 'no wonder; when they swill down all the floors of the brewery and cellars with town's water and wash casks with it'. One is left wondering what water was usually used to wash the casks.

It is interesting to note that the partners spend a lot of time discussing the financing of people to take off-licence shops, lending money to enable the borrower to purchase the ingoing and goodwill of an established business on condition that all beer was purchased from the firm.

In return for a loan of £20, trade of up to two or three barrels weekly could be secured. Most of these shops were run by married women whose husbands were at work. Bottled beer had not yet been established in the consumer's mind and a jug of beer to greet the homecoming labourer with his evening meal was customary. The quality of piped water had still to be accepted by ordinary folk, so beer on tap from the nearest off-licence was significant trade.

20 April 1881

There was indignation that Monro had ordered saccharin of indifferent quality from London, a substance then permissible to be used in the brewing process.

24 June 1881

They were taken aback that samples of porter sent to the county hospital had been returned without remark; the hospital was a steady customer.

28 June 1881

George Peckitt took over the Wigginton Mill Inn at Wigginton Bar, a mixed pub and farm business. On 30 June he was reported by the police for summons for being drunk on the premises along with the customers; he was given notice to leave by the brewery. His was a very serious offence because the licence was given to the licensee personally and not to the house, with forfeiture by the justices resulting in that house becoming delicensed – the law was to change later. On 2 July Inspector Hutchinson withdrew the charges against him. The partners felt obliged to follow suit in their action — they cancelled the notice.

Reginald Parker gave his London address twice in the diary (30 Queensgate SW) and departed. His colleagues used the opportunity to draw one another's attention to their respective errors, with a series of indignant entries; Parker's presence had a restraining influence. In the middle of July Monro also left for London, to 32 Curzon Street W. Those remaining continued their collective fault-finding; one of them read the diary entries back to the beginning of the year and found no action on various matters. The rent ledger had not been kept up to date, bills of sale were missing and no one knew what rent some tenants were supposed to be paying. They found that three of Melrose's houses, let to them at £150 a year, yielded them only £90 total rent; this provoked a frenzy.

7 July 1881

A tenant, Anne Johnson, came into the office and, though owing money on both trading and rent accounts, asked for a discount on supplies. Investigation by them revealed more horrors; she had paid only one third of her rent for the past five and a half years.

8 July 1881

They ordered two tons of rice from Mr Mills at £11 4s a ton. Why should they need so much rice in a brewery?

12 July 1881

A bad day. Since they had been in business the partners had been trying to recover a debt from James Green and now he had died on them. They decided to have a go at his son, Javan Green, on the assumption that he would have inherited his father's worldly possessions. To their dismay they discovered that he had made another will and that only his solicitors had got anything out of it. They read Monro's report on his visits to houses before he left; it too was dismal — the beer was all wrong in most of them.

18 July 1881

Parker returned, and the complaints about the beer flooded in. Their best tenant came into the office and said the beer was so awful he had lost all his customers, who had gone to a nearby John Smith's house. He was asked to return his beer at once. The most likely cause of the trouble would have been the spread of infection in the brewery during hot weather, and wild yeast penetrating the wort; it was not cured as a seasonal hazard until the improvements in brewing techniques and the growth of knowledge of the fermenting process in the 1950s.

The partners whiled away the anxious summer days with calculations in the diary. One was interesting; they calculated that a barrel of AK ale at 30 shillings wholesale price, selling at one penny a glass (half pint), would yield a gross profit of 18s 8d. A little consideration of this figure, taking into account ullage, shows it could only be valid if less than half a pint were sold each time, into a brim measure glass, with the reuse of the slops.

They calculated that 26 empty barrels weighed one ton and five full barrels also one ton; they then went into inconclusive figure work on the cost of carriage charged by the railway company.

1 August 1881

It was noted that the season was so dry that barges had been held up on the river wharf for weeks, waiting for a flood to move them higher up the river.

2 August 1881

Mrs Hembrough, tenant of the Paragon Inn, Cattle Market, York, was fined 40s by the justices for purchasing braces from soldiers, who then used the money to buy beer from her. The brewery traveller understood that on the previous Thursday she had married a man called Hardcastle — believed to be the same person who had been before the justices more than once and been fined for being in her house out of licensing hours — a short, pithy tale of contemporary morals along the lines of *The Beggar's Opera*.

The partners were still pursuing the matter of better brewing water; they had some samples from Tadcaster analysed.*

* This is the last entry until November 1882, when they started a new book. This they began with the best of intentions, for they proposed to index its contents for easy reference. The resolution lasted for nine pages only and was abandoned.

9 November 1882

A lot had happened that the diary sadly missed. A piece of land was purchased from the North Eastern Railway Company adjoining the road from Tadcaster to Boston Spa and next to George Hudson's abandoned railway line and bridge over the wharf to York. They built a brewery there during the summer of 1882 and ran a spur railway line into the brewery yard. They had arrived in the heartland of Yorkshire brewing to join four other breweries. The George Street, York brewery closed and became a depot and warehouse, and it remained the head office of the firm. Brewing began in the autumn. The partnership changed — Henry Lloyd retired and sold his share to the Honourable Geoffrey Nicholas Dawnay. The name of the firm changed too; it became the Tadcaster Tower Brewery Company.

9 November 1882

They noted that there was no weighing machine at the Tadcaster brewery and that they had no spare to send over. It was the first mention in the remaining volumes of the diary of the new brewery's existence.

10 November 1882

A partner noted that the tenant of the Spread Eagle, Walmgate, York, had given his notice to leave because of a letter he had received from Reginald Parker.

11 November 1882

There was a note in Parker's hand that the tenant had been pacified at 10.30 a.m. (precisely timed) and had been paid £24.

15 November 1882

Dawnay noted in the diary that he would be at 39 Berkeley Square, London until the following Monday.

17 November 1882

Parker reported a set-to with the Pulleyns of the Newcastle Arms, York, and stated that they were fearfully impudent and had refused to take another public house from the company. Parker had sent them away and threatened to clear them and their belongings out at a month's notice. It looked like the beginning of a fine dispute.

18 November 1882

They took stock of the brewery beer cellar; it held:

Treble X (best mild) 29 barrels
BA (ordinary bitter) 23 barrels and 17 kilderkins
KK (strong ale) 2 barrels and 9 kilderkins
with 30 barrels of X (mild) coming in.

This indicated, as might be expected, that the greatest trade was in mild beer and ordinary bitter (all around the same price); the strong ale reflected the custom of the time to brew small quantities of very strong ale for the cold weather, often drunk by putting a hot poker from the tap room fire into the glass before consuming.

20 November 1882

On an application by the brewery traveller to have the licence of the Reindeer, York, transferred to him, objection was made by Chief Constable Hayley, who stated in court that the next time a brewery traveller made such an application he would oppose it because the brewery was only using the traveller as a stopgap when it could not find a tenant; the police were advancing the arguments that licensees should be both resident on the premises and be considered permanent – rapid switching of licensees disturbed the police and non-resident licensees were anathema to them. There was a deal of sense in their attitude, but it was not enshrined in licensing law. Parker knew this and considered their stance 'a piece of officious impudence', and he doubted if the justices could refuse to transfer a licence.

25 November 1882

It was noted that Hayley was prepared to consent to McAndrew staying in the Bay Horse, Walmgate, York for a further week so long as the brewery made it right with the excise, and went on to say that he had found 40 to 50 people lying drunk on the floor and that the tenant had tried to bribe him with ten shillings; obviously the tenant was being required to leave at once, but the brewery could not find anyone to take over at such short notice – hence the week's grace. Also, it should have given Parker pause for reflection, for the relationship with the police was, as always, a two-way matter.

The partners aired their opinions on brewing, with particular regard to the acceptability of their own product; they felt the flatness of their beer arose entirely from it not being boiled either long enough or strongly enough; the general agreement was that it should be fiercely boiled during the last 20 minutes. The reference was to the preparation of the wort, being the boiled admixture of water and malt.

A few days later the diary was filled with complaints received from customers and partners about the new brewings at Tadcaster; customers were complaining 'loudly'. The partners said every brewing was half boiled (a change of innovation from being half baked), and the beer was full of yeast; they had not a barrel fit to sell. All this had the ring of a traditional attitude about beer; whenever there is a change in where or how beer is produced, even if it is really bad, the replacement is always worse. Hammonds' Brewery of Bradford, which ultimately bought Tadcaster Tower Brewery, brewed beer at its Fountain Brewery, which in local folklore was third on a scale of comparison, namely that there was good beer, bad beer and Hammonds' beer. In the 1950s they greatly improved the partners' Tadcaster Brewery, closed the Bradford brewery and brewed there. Were the citizens of Bradford grateful? No, a resounding No! And why? Because it did not taste like Hammonds' Fountain Brewery beer. But they didn't like Bradford beer? 'That's nowt to do wi' argument, just tain't t' same.'

29 November 1882

The partners were considering appointing a cooper, and they had at least six applicants from Sheffield, Leeds, Barrow in Furness and Northampton; the wages were 30 shillings a week.

30 November 1882

A private soldier of the 5th Dragoon Guards came from the

barracks and ordered two tins (jugs) of beer for trial; Parker saw him and made a present of them, and noted the soldier said the canteen ale was fearful. Perhaps Parker might well have silently put the firm's beer into the same category.

The chief constable was still waging war; he stopped one of the brewery's tenants from getting a licence, and told him to lock up his bar and cellar for good measure.

12 December 1882

Parker settled his dispute with Pulleyn, who called and signed his tenancy agreement. He was 'quite submissive'.

20 December 1882

A curious entry — 'Outward and Visible Signs by no means create an Inward and Spiritual Grace in our tenants – they will none of them have them and say "Good Beer is Sign Enough".' Was this an unexpected religious diversion or a refusal by the tenants to have any signboards on their premises – a common objection by licensees? They would tolerate a board giving the name of the pub, but would refuse one with the name of the brewery on it. This custom persisted well into the twentieth century, with only the big breweries putting their names on their pubs; the small ones did not.

Mrs Blakey was the housekeeper at the George Street offices and cooked for the partners' luncheons. An entry stated 'Mrs Blakey is having an allowance of three pints per day, the same as working men. This is ridiculous – a pint would be ample'. Parker told Clarke, the office manager, to allow this, adding 'it must not be forgotten that she has anything left daily from the partners' lunch besides.'

Parker went on to note down the beer stock, and that he had given the cooper notice to leave, and that a new cooper should be advertised for; his address was written down – the family home of Shirburn Castle, Tetsworth, Oxfordshire. He left for a break and left the problems of the business to the rest of them.

The head cooper waited until he had gone and told the partners he did not need another cooper and could do the work better without one.

Several entries appeared about the iniquity of the gas company digging holes all over York and blocking people's drains; the partners were exercised about this and discussed what could be done by way of legal action.

2

The Learning Process, 1883–1887

1 January 1883

There was, perhaps, a reference back to the note on signs – signboards were to be sent out to the tenants whether or not they wanted them. One entry recorded a signboard being sent as a New Year's present. Did the tenant really expect this as a New Year gift?

4 January 1883

Dundas noted in the diary that his address from 6 January to 17 March would be c/o Gillanders, Arbuthnot & Company, Calcutta.

Monro stated he had seen Joseph Firth at the brewery and had arranged that all steam pipes should be lagged with hair felt guaranteed to save 25 per cent steam. A man ahead of his time was Monro and, one might suspect, infuriating to the others. There was no question ever of him consulting them; they were told what he had been doing.

19 January 1883

They considered an invitation from W. H. Smith & Sons to subscribe for advertising cards to be hung in 50 railway stations; size 4' 4" x 2' 10" at £2 2s per annum.

In February old Mr Hotham (he was then 80 years old) called

for his rent money of £700. Meantime Monro had appealed against the rating assessment on the new brewery and got it reduced from £350 to £242 – a saving of £20 per annum in rates paid, at 4s 5d in the pound, according to him. His mathematics were approximate, but the principle was sound. Monro was the partner in charge of the brewery, in modern parlance the production director, with a self-given remit to interfere across the entire spread of the business.

They looked at their printed tenancy and furnished house agreements and felt that these did not meet their needs. They consulted their solicitor (Crombie) and a barrister (Gale), both of whom advised new agreements should be drawn.

They studied the purchase of wines and spirits by their tenants over several years; gloomily they came to the conclusion that the tie was being broken in many cases; one instance was a failure to buy any such stock for three years.

15 February 1883

Matthews, the tenant of the North Eastern Hotel, called in to see them and to report, with some acerbity, that trade was not what it was represented to him to be when he took the tenancy. The only comment in the diary is 'it is more likely to be worse', by an unknown hand. Cold comfort indeed, if that was what he was told.

During February Monro and Parker visited many of their houses; as the most active, inquisitive and vocal of the partners it must have been a *tour de force*. They discovered, again, that the fabric was crumbling, many needed painting, some were filthy, drains were often blocked, the beer was atrocious and only in a minority could they give a clean bill of health. At the Britannia, Walmgate, York, they found the place alive with vermin.*

A note in the diary recorded that they were receiving quite a number of applications from butlers and footmen for tenancies, instancing Dawnay's butler at Beningbrough and T. S. Kennedy's butler at Meanwood. Seemingly, the training was in the right direction; it might be wondered why there was a desire to switch a

* Since the diary began in 1879 not one of the partners had succeeded in spelling the name 'Britannia' correctly — they always spelled it with two 't's.

comfortable position for the rough and tumble of a public house — the level of pay and long hours of servitude?

28 February 1883

They took on a new traveller for the free trade, Poole, from Darlington. The agreed terms of employment were £150 a year, three months' notice on either side, and commission of 2.5 per cent on cash received up to £500 per annum, 3.5 per cent up to £1000 and 5 per cent above that figure. Bad debts would go against this commission.

20 March 1883

General pleasure was expressed about Monro's successful appeal against the brewery's rating assessment. The gross assessment had apparently been reduced to the level of the rateable value and, by way of explanation, it was noted that the latter was achieved by deducting 15 per cent from the gross rental value. Perhaps they were still baffled, as were later generations, by the arcane mysteries of rating law and practice.

5 April 1883

They noted that they had already paid £1100 to Walker, the building contractor for the new brewery, and felt that they should have a detailed statement for such an enormous sum. On the same day they fuelled their collective rage by learning that there were four maltsters on the strength and not one steeping of barley during the whole week. What was more, Mills's barley was in such stinking condition that Monro had never seen such filth. Monro, ever active, ever abrasive, ordered 20 quarters of Californian barley at 49 shillings.

10 April 1883

Monro lectured those who cared to listen. He was of the opinion that cask washing at Tadcaster was a myth — blowing steam through them did not clear them one little bit and, what was more, only split the staves. He suggested new ways of cask cleaning and wound up the lecture by writing 'they [the partners] should consider to be told that one of their casks was a stinker, was as great an injury to their feelings as to be told they had not washed themselves'.

He also reported that he had been told by Reed & Company of London that they had travellers paid by salary and no commission, who found full-time employment selling round about and only where they could deliver. The travellers came in every night and they never gave them any trouble. They kept 22 horses and their chief trade was free trade – and their beers were moderate. This was an interesting commentary – was it true? There has never been a solely salaried yet capable brewery sales force, for salesmen thrive on incentive. However, in its heyday from 1850 to 1950, when licensees demanded their beer, Bass could afford to have representatives on the road who went round testing the quality of the beer in the pubs and bestowing goodwill and patronage on the trade in general – much as Guinness did between and after the wars. The essential equipment of a Bass traveller was not an order book, but a bowler hat, a folding sample glass kept in his greatcoat pocket and a chauffeur-driven motorcar to conduct him round his calls. Even a third of a pint sample glass added up to a lot of beer in the course of a day. The Bass man, like the Guinness man, did not consider himself a vulgar traveller and pedlar of beer; he was far too superior for that. He condescended to accept orders from begging customers and there was no nonsense about discounts and, what was more, if he called and pronounced the beer was not being kept properly, then the licensee was struck off the list for future supplies. The system worked very well so long as there were plenty of free houses, local brewers unable to brew consistently good beer and, perhaps also, customers who appreciated good ale. All these factors vanished forever in the 1950s, and those two companies fell from their pedestals until rescued and given another role in the beer and liquor world. Colossi again, yes, but not with quite the same hauteur.

Monro dug into the activities of public-house brokers – agents who concentrated on finding prospective tenants for brewers – and in particular a man named Acton who was employed by the partners to find them tenants and temporary managers. What concerned him was that Acton never accounted for any profit to them for his activities on their behalf. Parker suggested they should surcharge the beer supplies to adjust for this forgetfulness on Acton's part. One must assume that when a house became empty, the partners, in desperation, begged Acton to find someone to keep it open, to preserve the licence, and at the same time kept up supplies of beer to the outlet, not invoicing anyone for them, in gratitude to Acton for taking a problem off their backs. Acton sold the beer, paid the temporary manager and kept what was left over. The entry demonstrated the primitive state of the partners' administration in what they considered an exceptional situation. The use of licensed house brokers was not widespread in the North, whereas it was common practice in the London area and continues to this day as a conduit for the recruitment of tenants. In the North the brewers developed their own facilities in their own offices with their own staff to engage new tenants and to deal with the procedures for installing them in houses; they also quickly spread this ability to the running of houses under direct management for profit, while London brewers looked askance on management falling along the way into the hands of powerful tenants with multiple tenancies of their houses. Only in the 1960s did they wake up to the realization that they were losing good profits for the sake of a smooth life.

On 12 March the office ink supply ran out and pencil was used in the diary entries until 23 April.

21 April 1883

The partners decided to put another traveller on the road in addition to Poole. They had agents in most of the big centres of population in the Northeast, including Darlington, Wakefield, Harrogate, Grimsby and Newcastle-upon-Tyne – in fact most of their free-trade beer was sold through agents. James Pullan was the Harrogate agent, and bought beer from them at 22 per cent discount up to £2000 purchases, and 22.5 per cent above; all orders were sent by rail, carriage free to the agent. In return, he paid for supplies in cash two months from the end of the month in which the deliveries were made and gave two substantial securities of £250 each.

On 1 April the partners received 132 cwts of hops; the English were Clements, Jenners, Hills and Conynghams – foreign hops were Bavarian (1880), Pops (1882), Altmarks (1882), Burgundian (1882) and Bavarian (1882).

They were very litigious as a firm, perhaps their upbringing giving them the inbuilt feeling of self-righteousness; the diary has constant reference to the law – evictions, putting in the bailiffs, levying distress, executing on goods, distraint, going to the Leeds assizes on various civil actions and appearing before the justices for infringements of the licensing laws. One after another, the names of solicitors consulted appear in the pages.

3 May 1883

An entry on cask purchase – 'New casks bought since brewing at Tadcaster 36 gallons – 300; 18 gallons – 300; 9 gallons – 100; 6 gallons – 100; total – 800.' This indicated trade must have been increasing for them since their move to Tadcaster; an unusual cask size was the six-gallon one. Also, no hogsheads (54 gallons), the badge of the really big and powerful brewer.

7 May 1883

They pasted into the diary an extract from *The Times* newspaper, which was a report of a case heard in the Queen's Bench Division of the High Court involving the firm, and concerning the forfeiture of a licence of a public house they owned at Wetherby. The tenant had made an internal communication between the public house and adjoining unlicensed premises, which was without consent previously obtained, against the law and a heinous offence. The licence was forfeited by the justices. The legal argument was a lawyer's paradise, but the partners were granted their application – a mandamus requiring Quarter Sessions to hear the case again.

19 May 1883

There was a note about beer stocks being too large, followed by a riposte with chapter and verse concerning monthly sales, mainly BA (53 barrels), KK (26 barrels), and the argument ceased.

19 May 1883

Henry Whitehead, of the Thirteen Bells (an unusual name), Kirkgate, Leeds, signed an agreement to commence as the firm's traveller in Leeds. The partners were so pleased with this stroke of good fortune that they undertook to pay one half of an unspecified guarantee.

24 May 1883

Monro intervened. He had ascertained that Whitehead was a first-class traveller and 'must on no account be employed by this firm'. Very curious.

25 May 1883

The mandamus hearing date before Quarter Sessions was known; Monro wrote this into the diary in red ink and guaranteed the legal costs of the firm. Quite obviously, he was nervous about committing the partners to a very expensive law case and, to allay their fears, wrote further, in red ink, the legal significance of it to them.

26 May 1883

Parker and Dundas told Milner to refuse to guarantee Whitehead. They had found out that he had been to prison five times.

29 May 1883

Monro delivered another lecture. Pasted into the diary was a disquisition against the overstocking of running (popular low-gravity) ales in the summertime on account of the risk of acidity, the locking up of capital in stock and casks, and, because ales intended to be consumed quickly could use lower tap neats, making a more saccharine, less dextrinous beer and thus obtaining a fuller palate in a cheaper beer — all in all a very technical explanation covering a whole foolscap page. The others must have been struck dumb, for there is no reply.

31 May 1883

Just once, someone spelt 'Britannia' correctly; it did not last, for on 2 June they were back to their old habit.

At the beginning of June Monro departed for 32 Curzon Street, London, but was soon back, as on 29 June there was an entry by him. Were the partners 'aware that Amos [the brewery foreman] had 22 men on last week', that is, while he was away.

They got back at him immediately, by changing the battle ground – a long entry on the likely cost of the mandamus proceedings; they pointed out it was likely to set him back £30.

22 June 1883

Parker had had enough; he was going off to Morpeth for a few days. On 19 June the mandamus case had been heard and the result noted in the diary. The partners had the licence of the Star, Wetherby restored, but no costs were allowed against the justices; a Pyrrhic victory.

There was an undated entry by Monro. He wrote a list of tenants whom he considered had outstanding rent and goods accounts, with the adjuration that 'these matters must be looked into'.

27 June 1883

The partners offered to pay the rents for the tents any of their tenants had taken on the Knavesmire. This was a reference to beer tents for the races.

6 July 1883

Monro took his red ink and penned a warning that 'stocks were too large, the beer would go sour before it was drunk up'. He also noted that no intoxicating liquor licences would be granted for the Knavesmire.

24 July 1883

They sent for a Mr Edwards to see them at noon on Saturday and promised to pay his railway expenses in connection with setting up an agency in Huddersfield.

28 July 1883

The tenant of the White Swan came in and 'was most insolent', refusing to buy any beer from them as he was not tied. They could not find his tenancy agreement and suspected Monro had lost it.

30 July 1883

Amos came into the office and complained that he could not keep five painters at work. Monro gave an immediate answer – get rid of three. Then George Fowler, of Leeds, applied for a tenancy. It was noted that he had lived with Lord Vivian, Lord Harewood and Mr Montague for four and a half years and that Colonel Gunter knew him. The application was dismissed abruptly – someone wrote over the entry 'Won't do; drinks'.

31 July 1883

Monro was convinced that the beer sent by rail was being tapped and that they were losing three 36-gallon cask equivalents in every 100 sent, because four people at Tadcaster brewery knew the casks left full, and yet they arrived at their destinations six to nine gallons short. An early example of staff shrinkage.

10 August 1883

Concern was expressed that beer samples were constantly being drunk up by the men in the George Street depot. So it was decided to lock the samples in the old brewhouse.

An entry appeared for the first time and ran for several weeks; Monkman, of Pocklington, a tenant, was in grave danger of losing his licence by forfeiture. With the mandamus case fresh in their minds, they worried in the diary about the matter. It was suggested that Monro should be dispatched to deal with it.

The free-trade debt list was examined; Crombie, the solicitor, was given instructions to recover some £80 worth, on a commission basis of 10 per cent for every debt under £3 collected, 5 per cent for £5 and over, plus disbursements.

27 August 1883

A newspaper report was pasted into the diary about the Brewster Sessions meeting of the Burnley Licensing Justices at which a petition signed by over 15,000 people, or one quarter of the population of Burnley, protested against the application for renewal of a grocer's [off-]licence. The partners were very worried about this movement against beer off-licence shops, which temperance folk and others perceived as causing poverty, misery and crime among the labouring classes, and with some element of truth. The Temperance Movement was a product of the Lancashire mill towns, where the effects of drunkenness were apparent in every street.

28 August 1883

Monro had obtained the opinions of two solicitors on the validity of serving a notice to quit on Hornsea with regard to his tenancy.

The mandamus proceedings in connection with the Star, Wetherby, were not over. Notice was received that the renewal of the licence would be opposed. A whole page was taken up with the partners writing down their views on this and the legal right of the justices to refuse a renewal; gloomily, they came to the conclusion that they would not win again.

31 August 1883

Monro was of the opinion that they needed an office boy at five shillings a week to copy letters, tick off gyles (beer brewing batch numbers) and deal with the *Cask Book*, instead of employing a man at £1 a week who spent half his time running errands and delivering telegrams and letters.

4 September 1883

Monro testily enquires why it is necessary to open an account with Boby, whose product was no better, when the existing supplier of finings, Boke, had supplied finings to their entire satisfaction for some time past.

7 September 1883

They were concerned that the Duke of Devonshire would be onto them about the urinal at the Castle Vaults, Knaresborough, leased from the Devonshire estate and noted that Charles Powell was his grace's solicitor.

Monkman came into the office stinking 'like a stoat' and drunk as well. Monro promised to attend to this matter personally on 22 September.

On the same day, Lord Harewood, sitting as chairman of Wetherby Petty Sessions, refused to renew the licence of the Star,

Wetherby, on the basis that it was not needed for the neighbourhood, nor was it structurally adapted as a public house. The partners considered Monro's undertaking about legal costs.

22 September 1883

A plaintive entry – 'Where is Barnes Whitwell's lease?' Written underneath – 'Found'. The system of filing in the office left much to be desired; but there was no caustic comment from Monro.

10 October 1883

Monro wanted to know why, with all the painters employed by the partnership, PW should be employed to mend the windows. The partners could arrange for their own employees to do the glazing and save 75 per cent of the cost – all joiners could glaze, according to Monro.

18 October 1883

Three employees were sacked for stealing beer.

20 October 1883

The partners suggested certain terms of employment for the free-trade traveller, Hagley. Monro was against the terms, being quite certain they would not pay off, and in any case he was not in favour of taking him on.

7 November 1883

Monro saw Mrs Eccles, tenant of the Sun, Tanner Row, York, about her permitting drunkenness on the premises, and from the entries in the diary subsequently, he persisted so effectively that she left on 9 November at 10.00 a.m.

16 November 1883

There was a note that the mare being driven by Cook in the light cart was so frightened by a trap passing that she set to kicking, throwing Cook over her head into the road; the cart was smashed and the mare hurt her knee. There was nothing about Cook's condition.

17 November 1883

There was a postdated entry to the effect that at Quarter Sessions the company had applied to renew the Star licence and had got it. The cost was £24.

William Johnson of The Mount, Chapel Allerton, Leeds, was set on as a brewery agent at 30 shillings a week, plus commission.

20 November 1883

Newbold, a tenant, and his wife, came to the office to see if he could get a reduction in his rent from £30 to £25 a year. Both assured the partners that they never put any liquor (water) in the brandy, but sold it as received from the brewery. Whereupon it was suggested to them that by adding one pint to each gallon, they would soon gain the £5 a year reduction they wanted!

23 November 1883

Stephenson, in charge of the horses, had been so drunk that he could not work even after three days had passed, so he was sacked and Dixon put in his place.

A few days later the partners reduced all the carters' wages by three shillings a week, and instead allowed them commission on empty casks and jugs brought back to the brewery. It was noted that there had been a perceptible difference already in the numbers of empty vessels returned.

They returned to attacking the railway company about freight charges; they demanded reduced rates because of the increase in trade. The railway company refused to budge.

28 November 1883

They considered their free trade and came to the conclusion that it was not worth the candle after allowing discounts of one sort and another, and that it would be better to let it go to Smith, be paid out by him and have done with it.

12 December 1883

There was a heavy gale and resulting damage to several roofs of York houses, stripping tiles and blowing down chimneys.

13 December 1883

Monro walked out to Bishopthorpe to the Ebor and found that the tenant was in fact living at Leeds, and was a drayman for Tetleys. He had left his father as manager for him. Monro returned hot-foot to the office to deal with this.

On the same day W. H. Robson, of Hornsea, Hull, was appointed agent for Hull and district.

The partners moved into state of the art technology — they purchased a rubber stamp entitled 'Tadcaster Tower Brewery Company', and it was relentlessly used thereafter in the diary.

20 December 1883

An entry in red ink showed Monro had discovered that the county court action against Wright had 'entirely broken down', and that the libel case of Wright versus Monro was 'assumimg very large proportions'. Monro went to Scarborough and stayed all actions, both of his own and of the firm's, by paying Wright £25 from his private purse. He was not on the winning side for once.

27 December 1883

They went through the free-trade travellers' list of 40 customers to whom they wished to send Christmas boxes and, after carefully comparing the list with the ledger, cut the number to 14, to each of whom they sent a nine-gallon cask of XXX best mild.

31 December 1883

Parker called at the York Conservative Club to see if he could get some trade, but the secretary said there were so many interested in the trade who were mixed up with the club that they would all expect a turn. Parker then saw the club manager and suggested a commission of 5 per cent on all orders. Apparently, in the past six months only one kilderkin of ale had been purchased from the firm; as a final bribe Parker gave the manager ten shillings as a Christmas box.

Bribery and corruption of customers' employees to obtain trade was rife and expected until very recent years. In the 1970s the police in south Yorkshire began to take an interest in the practice from a criminal point of view and threatened prosecution of the committee members of large working men's clubs and the breweries involved. This led to undertakings of reputable behaviour, and the scale of presents and incentives being defined by the brewery companies, and the affair died down. At the same time a drive took place against generous Christmas presents, particularly to police officers, and the wanton dimension which hitherto had prevailed abated, never to return to such generosity.

* * *

The year 1884 began with Parker going to see Mr Hunter of Messrs Hunter & Smallpage, the well-known York furnishing firm, at the shop of Mr Sowray, a chemist. They were trustees for a Mr Tonge, the owner of the freehold of the White Swan, Goodramgate, York, a very old coaching inn. There was much involved discussion as to the worth of the freehold reversion to the partnership lease, and the price the trustees wanted for it. Appropriately, Parker was suitably outraged and astonished at their greed and departed to report back to his colleagues. What was interesting was the decision of the trustees to act on their own advice in a trust matter, unless, indeed, it was merely a preliminary skirmish.

2 January 1884

The partners looked at their sales for the last quarter of 1883 and compared them with those for 1882. They were depressed to find that their sales of wines and spirits had decreased from £3564 to £3356; obviously Melrose was still at it. They cheered up at finding the sales of beer stood at 113,419 gallons, against 75,230; the decision to move the brewing to Tadcaster must have been a substantial cause of the rise, plus Monro's energy in all fields.

3 January 1884

A cutting from the *Standard* newspaper was stuck into the diary; it was a letter to the editor from the clerical superintendent of the executive committee of the Church of England Temperance Society, stating that a bill would be introduced into Parliament in the forthcoming session to rescind the existing privileges extended to grocers and shopkeepers to sell retail spirits. The society felt that if it became law it would strike a blow at the root of female intemperance, which was considered to be the contemporary scourge of the working classes. The fact that the partners took note of this movement disturbed them, but they, like the rest of the licensed trade, did not know how to combat it; keeping a low profile and their mouths shut was the favoured tactic.

4 January 1884

Parker went by rail from York to Church Fenton, where they had the Railway Hotel. He was appalled by the dilapidated state of the property. He went on to Tadcaster, where the brewer reported getting good extracts from the malt. He also learned about the new method of dealing with stinking casks. His main purpose, however, was to institute a new bookkeeping system.

5 January 1884

He was outraged to have a cheque drawn on the Knaresborough & Claro Banking Company by a free-trade customer rejected; Matthews, the traveller, was wired for an explanation.

7 January 1884

He learned that the tenant of the Bridge, Layerthorpe, had done a moonlight flit. He went round and the house was closed. The police were informed and reported the tenant was 'holed up' in the Balcony, Piccadilly, York. Parker set off again and found his wife there, astonished that they had been discovered; she promised that her husband would bring in the key to the office and sign over the licences. It turned out to be a bad debt; the tenant had nothing.

There was better news later in the day — the partners obtained possession of the Ebor Hotel, Bishopthorpe, from Peter Austin Wake; and the man who had delivered the bounced cheque put his account in funds and it was met.

8 January 1884

One of the brewery travellers came into the office and reported that the customers were very satisfied with the beers.

Monro entered 1884 with vigour; he recorded in the diary that owing to the partners being slow to give an answer to his request of 20 December, the firm had lost the mortgage on the house at Rothwell to Tetley, that is, a tied loan to the free-house owner. There was another year of lecturing in store for the rest of them.

9 January 1884

The justices refused to transfer the licence of the Tiger, York, to George Giles because they understood the woman living with him was not his wife. Parker had to wire the vicar of the church in Manchester for a copy of the marriage certificate.

On the same day Monro said they could purchase the Drover's Arms, Riccall, which he commended on the basis that they could close it and get all the trade of the village into the Greyhound, which they already owned. The other partners quickly squashed this suggestion, pointing out, inconsequentially in view of the facts they adduced at the same time, that the Greyhound was in very poor order and its trade dropping every year. Monro riposted with his own note in the diary that his idea was sustainable, but the matter went no further. Buying up other public houses in a neighbourhood and shutting them was a familiar ploy by brewers, bred out of long years of the monopoly licensing system. It distorted accepted principles of competition and inculcated a certain way of thinking in brewers about the meaning of competition, and stimulating restrictive administrative procedures to the detriment of customer satisfaction, variety and initiative, both in themselves and their tenants. It was a cramping and narrow attitude, which has continued to the present day.

Giles, of the Tiger, finally admitted he was not married; nothing more was recorded, but presumably the justices refused him his licence transfer and he disappeared into history.

10 January 1884

Parker went to Escrick and saw Lord Wenlock. His lordship praised the firm's beer and went on to state that if the quality was maintained he would purchase all his requirements from them. Parker then proceeded to see the butler and got an order for seven hogsheads – surely for the hall and estate employees, Lord Wenlock's capacity being not up to such a quantity.

The partners wrote up their comments on the shortage of casks and each had his own ideas about where they were.

16 January 1884

Parker drove over to Stockton on Forest and saw Mrs Metcalfe, tenant of the Rose & Crown, and found her very much the worse for drink. He persuaded her, after a long discussion, that it was time she gave up the tenancy. In the evening of the same day, after returning to York, he received word from her son-in-law that she had been found dead at the bottom of the staircase.

21 January 1884

The partners for many years had the advertisement space above the leader column in the *York Herald* and were distressed to find the newspaper had removed it to another page. The matter was taken up with the manager, who was very contrite and promised to restore the status quo at once.

24 January 1884

They considered the ten quarters of Smyrna barley purchased for malting and were pleased to find it yielded 86.9 pounds a quarter – far beyond their expectations. On 22 January they had thought about appointing an agent in Sheffield, and had two candidates, Parkin and Westoby. Westoby had worked for the Brunswick Brewery Company, a small brewery owned by the Chambers family. He felt he could sell 30 to 50 barrels a week. He told them that Smith of Tadcaster had as yet no agent in Sheffield.

30 January 1884

They took up a reference from Chambers, who highly recommended Westoby.

31 January 1884

They were concerned about hop prices, which were hardening; however, they thought they had enough in store. They noted that Smith of Tadcaster had bought 700 pockets (a pocket was a traditional measure of wool and hops and, in the latter case, a quantity of some 168 pounds).

4 February 1884

Parker attended a meeting of the Common Right Holders of Strensall, held at the Mansion House, York, at which many people were present. The meeting finally agreed to appoint a committee of six to meet Colonel Bland, the government agent, and to ask for £10,800 for the Common. The government had previously indicated that it would be establishing a military camp there.

6 February 1884

Caswell, the head brewer, came over from Tadcaster and they settled on a list of hop purchases. They felt they were all right for supplies until August.

The diary entries gave specific details of the partners' travels around the North of England. They used trains extensively; the widespread network of lines and regular service enabled them to cover a lot of calls in one day – especially if the local traveller or agent met them with his pony and trap – and be back home each evening. The same problems come up again and again – bad debts, bad beer, wayward and commercially inept tenants, public houses in poor repair and eccentric justices. The *York Herald* promised to give them publicity when they opened their office in Pavement, York, on 18 February, but it was touch and go whether the paper would do so. In the event it did.

The excellent railway system made it possible for them to send their beer all over the country. In February they sent samples of their Old Ale to David Robertson & Company in London and their pressed yeast for sale to Dawson of Glasgow. Apart from the continuing limiting effect of the restrictive licensing laws on the brewery trade, modern rail transport opened up the market for them for a short time until the tied house system removed virtually all free houses.

Geoffrey Dawnay took some leave and went to Lismore, County Cork; he left his address.

27 February 1884

Parker wrote into the diary the journeys arranged for Kilburn, the York and district traveller. Three days a week were devoted to York and its markets and on the other three days he had to cover the villages within a ten-mile radius, plus Thirsk, Selby, Scarborough, Whitby and Pickering.

28 February 1884

A sergeant farrier of the 5th Dragoons came into the office to see about taking the tenancy of the Wheatsheaf, Hungate, York. He told them that the 21st Hussars would shortly be relieving the 5th Dragoons. They therefore wired the regimental sergeant major of the Hussars, then stationed at Cahin Island, soliciting his custom, sending price lists and a prepaid telegraph reply form, and asking for confirmation that they were coming to York.

29 February 1884

Westoby sent in his first order from Sheffield, for 13 hogsheads of BA; they sent him AK and marked it BA, charging the BA price!

1 March 1884

They received a telegraph from the 21st Hussars; they were not coming to York. The partners consoled themselves – they had never really believed it anyway.

8 March 1884

Lord Hawke's gamekeeper called. He wanted the tenancy of the Black Horse, Poppleton; the partners asked his lordship for a character reference.

24 March 1884

Trade was bad and the partners sought ways of reducing their overheads; they took the traditional line brewers always take – to reduce wages and neglect property repairs. They also could have reduced the strength of the beer and perhaps they did, but it was not recorded. The foreman of the works department, Amos, was asked what work was in progress. He stated that there were 33 jobs in hand, of which 17 were roof repairs. Parker told him that tenants must take their turn at repairs and that he would be demoted from foreman at £2 2s weekly to joiner at £1 15s. To get the roof repairs done, they would keep on the bricklayer at £1 10s weekly, the joiner at £1 9s 3d and a boy at 6 shillings.

Furthermore, Amos and the joiner, who were doing the carpentry, could also do some painting, as they were used to it in former jobs. Beyond that, they would put out some painting to Boynton, the tenant of the Victoria, leaving Amos to see that the job was done properly.

29 March 1884

Poole, the Darlington traveller, called in to apply for an increase in basic salary, which seemed to be £1 a week plus commission. He wanted £4 a week and would guarantee more trade. It might have been considered an inopportune time to make this request; Parker clearly thought so and filled six pages of the diary with calculations to prove that the partnership could not pay him, but ended by saying he was a good traveller. No conclusion was reached.

1 April 1884

Sales for the first quarter of the year were noted; 3352 gallons of wines and spirits against 2728 for the previous year, and 105,667 gallons of ale against 70,308.

3 April 1884

Westoby called in and reported that the beer was going down well in Sheffield and was well liked. He felt, however, that the BA ought to be a bit milder and that the XXX was too dark. So long as the beer was in good condition, he felt he could sell over 30 barrels a week. There were no observations on whether the beer drank its strength!

In the afternoon, Poole's son came over from Darlington with high praise for all the beers and went with Parker to Tadcaster to see the brewery and to select some XX for a new customer. There was a general note that all was going well and that the new stores were nearly finished, and were looking remarkably nice.

15 April 1884

The head brewer reported a mishap in the brewery. He had left the copper man to look after the boiling of the copper and gone to bed; the copper man had fallen asleep and let the copper boil over, and they lost 36.25 barrels. The partners were in no doubt what to do to compensate for the loss; the next few brews would be attenuated, and Levett, the copper man, was sent for and spoken to very sharply about his carelessness.

17 April 1884

Parker went to see Anderson & Lythe, agents concerned with the sale of Oldbridge's brewery. It was in the hands of the bank and, in addition to the brewery premises, had 15 tied houses and the goodwill of 11 leasehold houses; they wanted £22,000. Apparently, the deal was to see if the partners would be prepared to give financial assistance, in return for the right of supply to the houses. No deal was reached. It turned out that the brewery was sold to Watson of Selby.

5 May 1884

After many weeks of not being able to find a tenant for the White Swan, Goodramgate, York, the partners communicated with Rowbotham of London, licensed property valuers and brokers, giving details of the property, and received a reply with speed enough to cause suspicion, that they had the very person to take it — a Mr Bradbury. Overnight Rowbotham made enquiries and the next day telegraphed to ask if it was the White Swan, Pavement or Goodramgate, the former being an ancient coaching inn proper, and the latter, having lost its former glory as such, was coasting along as a rather rough alehouse. No more was heard from Rowbotham, and the partners were left with the house.

10 May 1884

They had a brainwave to make extra money — establish a company to market their surplus yeast for sale to bakers. The topic was enthusiastically discussed in the diary; that was as far as it went.

13 May 1884

Parker heard that Canon Randolph of Dunnington, where the firm owned the Blacksmith's Arms, was doing his best to have it closed. Like Henry II, Parker felt beset by a pestilent priest, and called upon him, explaining that the firm had a vested interest in the house, and (a nice touch) that it provided as much of a living for the tenant as the canon's preaching did for him. What was more, they would find a suitable tenant for the place. The canon protested that he had nothing against the public house being there.

20 May 1884

Parker found a tenant, Metcalfe, and (another nice touch) wrote to the canon asking about his character; but the wily cleric was not to be drawn. He replied that the man both drank and betted.

22 May 1884

Mr Pike of Reading wrote asking for samples of the firm's Old Ale, which was dispatched the same day.

D. Wake of Stillington, a tenant, and his stepson were reported to have been fighting; further, Wake had advertised that he would not be answerable for his wife's debts. A cryptic note in the diary recorded that the daughter of the family was mixed up with a doctor's assistant and that the 'whole thing was a muddle'. Parker noted that he would go over the following day to sort it out.

The military camps were opening for the season and the partners set off to tour the barracks soliciting trade; on 24 May they went to the canteen at the infantry barracks to see about orders, but came away empty handed. They were hopeful of wresting the supply contract for the prison and hospital from a London firm; they already supplied the lunatic asylum.

27 May 1884

The York tramway company had not paid its rent and the partners threatened it with a writ.

They continued their trade assault on the infantry barracks for the supply of beer; they were determined to get Simonds of Reading, and Brett and Flint of Manchester, as current suppliers, out.

29 May 1884

It was reported that Gowthorpe, of the Marcia, Bishopthorpe, had been summoned for serving travellers on a Sunday, who were not, in the view of the law, *bona fide* travellers. They were soldiers from Fulford, and for years the publican had always served these men on a Sunday afternoon. Apparently, some ten days earlier a dragoon had fallen into the Ouse and drowned while returning from Bishopthorpe by boat. Gowthorpe said that he had only served shandy gaff and that it had been proved at the inquest that he was sober when he got into the boat. Miss Milner had taken the matter up in the temperance cause and, in a letter to the newspapers, had suggested that the victim had taken beer at Bishopthorpe and that this had caused the accident. She was obliged to withdraw her allegation, but returned to the attack by suggesting that Bishopthorpe was not the minimum three miles from Fulford, the distance prescribed for travellers. This stirred the police into action, and they issued a summons to test the matter. This in turn provoked Gowthorpe to state that if he were stopped from serving *bona fide* travellers on a Sunday, then half his trade would disappear.

31 May 1884

Parker departed for St Paul's College, Cheltenham, and then went on to Somerset for a holiday. A few days later Dawnay went off to 37 Bury Street, St James's, London.

While they were away, Gowthorpe's case came up before the justices, who told him he was liable to prosecution if he supplied any York man under the guise of being a traveller, on a Sunday. But Gowthorpe was not to be cowed; he argued, and rightly according to Parker, that 'York Post Office was three miles and consequently anyone sleeping Saturday night the other side of the Post Office was a traveller.' It was undoubtedly a good argument, but nothing came of it.

The partners noted that 'feasts' had started again, and that they would continue their policy established two years previously of not contributing free beer — in fact, the custom ought to be stopped. Without any break in the diary entry, they stated that Mrs Blakey, their housekeeper at the George Street offices, got dirtier every day and must be exchanged for the Baker family: 'Mrs Blakey gets dirtier every day. Why not exchange her for the Baker family; they have four children, and one boy is in the Minster choir and surely the three others would not drink and consume as much as Mrs B's great sons, grandsons and cousins. Mrs Baker is a cook and, we understand, highly accomplished.'

The partners then went in for one of their periodic bouts of self-flagellation, covering several pages, vying with each other to reveal the worst property they owned – 'roof is in holes and must been seen to', 'Thompson of the Waggon & Horses was promised his roof would be repaired this spring – this must be attended to', 'paint front, back of house never been touched with paint'.

7 June 1884

Monro had Kaye, the manager of the North Eastern Hotel, into the office for a long time, and ended up with an order for five hogsheads of BA, to be sent to the Royal Station Hotel at 10.30 on Monday morning. They were trying to get Smith's beer out and theirs in.

The weather was warming up and so was the beer infection; the diary pages were filled with dire reports. Monro was back at the infantry barracks trying to replace Brett's beer.

9 June 1884

Monro was in form – 'the gyle book is perfectly disgraceful. I should say at least £300 worth of beers are not accounted for; X and XX brewed in March are not sent out, not to be found. I should say 150 casks in all, numbers are wrongly taken in every book and we might as well keep no books at all.' His red ink ran out and he goes on with blue for another paragraph.

10 June 1884

A defence swiftly appeared; someone waxed indignant at Monro's attack; it was plainly stated there were no casks in the gyle book of any size which were not accounted for, but there is an admission that Hammond, the brewer, should keep the book up to date.

11 June 1884

There was a reply from the Ashton Gate Brewery of Bristol stating that they appreciated the samples of Old Ale sent, but that they were too old for blending purposes.

12 June 1884

One of the partners wrote down all his visits for the day. He went from York to Easingwold, then to Craike, on to Stillington, round to Strensall and back to York; something like 30 miles by pony and trap. On the way out he had called in at the asylum at Clifton, enquired about the beer and received a further order. At the Angel, Easingwold, he inspected the repairs being done. At Craike, he called on the tenant and noted that the beer was in good condition. At the Bay Horse, Stillington, he made a note of some repairs the tenant requested, saw a customer in the house who was a joiner and asked for a price for the work. As the tenant had only recently moved in, he checked his licence and found that the excise licence had been lost, but the protection order preceding the grant of a full transfer of the licence was all right. He passed the opinion that the new tenant was just the man for the house. At the Ship, Strensall, he saw the tenant, who said summer business was good but that winter killed the benefit of it. The house looked in good order and was full of customers. However, he thought that the other house they owned in Strensall needed doing up, for although there were a good many soldiers in it, they looked rather dirty. He took the opportunity to tell the tenant to reduce his trade account debt immediately. He then went back to York. The next day he went over to Tadcaster.

14 June 1884

A letter from the senior commissariat officer stated that he had been directed by the secretary of state for war to acquaint the firm that he had accepted their tender for the supply of wines and spirits to the military hospital and prison for three years. This pleased them and they looked into the diary to remind themselves what prices they had quoted.

16 June 1884

Mrs Fowler of 8 Leeman Road, York, called in to say that she had given up the idea of applying for a licence for a house in Leeman Road and that she had brought the plans for the proposed public house with her and that they were welcome to them. The land on which the house was to be built belonged to Mr Harrison, a land surveyor of St John's Street, The Groves, York, and he wanted £90 for it. They wondered whether it would be worth their while to take up the matter and, instead of applying for a new licence, to transfer an existing licence if the justices would permit it. They thought their worst house was the Sun in Tanner Row. They did in fact pursue the matter of Mr Harrison's land in Leeman Road, where they built a public house in 1887 and called it the Jubilee.

17 June 1884

One of them went up to the barracks and learned from the adjutant that the colonel had given orders to discontinue the Manchester beers and to get supplies from the firm. The estimate of trade was 100 barrels a month. At the same time he learned that the 20th Hussars stationed in Ireland would be coming to York in August when the 5th Dragoons left. The partners were convinced that the Manchester brewers would have another go to try to get their beer in, so they had arranged for their own traveller to get in first. They had learnt that the wicked Brett was going over to Ireland to nobble the 20th Hussars for their beer supplies – hence the hurry to send Kilburn, their own traveller, over the next day.

18 June 1884

Parker decided to take a trip to South Teeside. He took a nine o'clock train from York to South Stockton, and was met by their agent. Together they went over to Boosbeck, and then to the New Inn at Skelton, to see the owner, who wanted to sell it. He recorded for the benefit of his partners that he liked neither the house nor its owner. They returned to Boosbeck, to the Commercial, where he berated the tenant about his overdue account, noting that while the house was very large, it was wretchedly furnished, and that close by streets of houses had collapsed through mining subsidence. He passed the observation that trade was nearly at a standstill and that groups of out-of-work men could be seen standing at every street corner. This was the centre of the iron mining industry, which in addition to poor trade was beginning to feel the effects of cheap iron-ore importation. He then walked from Boosbeck to Lendal and saw a free-trade customer whose wife complained that the beer was flat and dull. She refused to promise any more orders, but said that if they could guarantee that the beer would be right, she would order five or eight hogsheads the following week. Parker noted that the house was a good one; it was well furnished and did a good business. His noting of the trade was an indication of the level of consumption of beer in the mining villages then and until the 1960s. He took a train from Boosbeck to Saltburn by the Sea, and there visited the impressive Queen's Hotel. It was at a resort the railway company and others were trying to promote as a kind of northern Brighton. He felt it was too big, badly furnished and, worst of all, owed a lot of money on the trading account. He got a train to Darlington, where he called on another free-trade customer who was behind with his account. Finally, he went to see the agent's father, Poole, who comforted him with the news that trade was dreadful in the North. He returned to York that evening.

The next day, back in the office, Mr W. H. Wintle called upon him to enquire if the partners would subscribe anything towards the Hospital & Home for Incurables at Harrogate, for which he was secretary. Parker was too depressed by the previous day's visit and replied with his own enquiry. What was the hospital's trade in beer, wines and spirits and who had the business? Wintle replied that he was responsible for their orders and that if the partners subscribed he would be glad to deal with them. Parker promised two guineas so long as the greater proportion of the beer trade came to them; and this was agreed.

20 June 1884

The wife of the tenant (Saul) of the Three Cranes, Lendal, York, came in with their notice to give up the tenancy and said they were thinking of bringing an action against the firm for false misrepresentation about the trade of the house. She showed a list of their debts and Parker noticed they owed £110 to Smith of Tadcaster! In one of their tied houses!

23 June 1884

They received a telegram from Kilburn, who was with the 20th

Hussars in Ireland, asking for £5 to be sent to Cork to enable him to lobby the soldiers. It was noted in the diary that he had been given £5 for this purpose before he left York. The only message Kilburn had on trade prospects was that three breweries were in for the trade and that they might get a part.

24 June 1884

Parker had had enough. He went on holiday for the remainder of the week to Orde House, Morpeth.

26 June 1884

The partners had a bout of internal hysteria over free-trade debts; they did a lot of calculations and entered their handiwork in the diary, principally directed against the activities of their Northeast traveller, Poole Junior. There was a consensus that he had sold £4000 of beer over 16 months, but had accumulated £258 4s 9d of bad debt – the equivalent of 6.5 per cent of the sales. It was written in large letters 'THIS IS EXCEPTIONALLY HIGH'. A reason was sought for this and the conclusion was that trade 'was dreadful in the North'. They thought Poole was 'an arrant fool about not checking accounts before he took them on or doing anything to get them reduced once he had started'; or indeed, telling the partners the real position of his customers financially. They calmed down as the written analysis gave pause for reflection, and comforted themselves that perhaps he was sorting his customers out and that the position had improved from when he first began as a traveller. However, the general view was that he would have to be summoned to York for a serious talk. Nothing has really altered in 100 years – salesmen sell and the office tries to collect the cash; directions are issued, strict warnings thundered out, threats of non-supply made. A salesman is a salesman, not a walking credit controller, if for no other reason than that he is an optimist; obtaining the order is the triumph, the rest will follow – he hopes. In any case, the brewer is concerned to keep the mash tun filled and the beer flowing. Until accountants finally took over running breweries in the 1960s and tradition departed out of the window, the only brewer to local knowledge who ever refused to supply a recalcitrant paying customer was Tetley of Leeds; the others threatened to cut off supplies but did not implement their threats so long as the volume of trade was good. Tetley of Leeds was rather different — his beer was good, in popular demand and licensees needed it to attract their clientele. So if the previous order had not been paid for the next order was not delivered. What was more, he had only two qualities of beer — mild and bitter, in barrels or hogsheads; it was not even bottled until well into the twentieth century. Happy man, shrewd brewer, successful in his calling, he felt no need to own public houses until long after his rivals had secured their tied estates; only in the 1920s did his company feel the necessity to follow them. Having dominated the Leeds beer market in free trade, the company did the same with its pubs, and does so to this day. The partners, and their rivals in the Leeds area, had to use Tetley as their marker.

27 June 1884

Kilburn returned from his expedition to Ireland. He reported to the partners, who thought he might have got on the right side of the sergeant major, who had promised to do what he could with regard to the sergeants' mess. But the Lion Brewery in Leeds seemed to be the front runner for the business; the partners determined to keep at it though, with a desperate optimism. Kilburn told them that Brett of Manchester had not even bothered to attend the army in Ireland and had instead engaged in some shooting near Flagstone, and offered the NCOs as much shooting as they liked. The partners saw this as an underhand trick of the first order of infamy; also, they gathered that the 15 per cent discount they gave on their own supplies to military canteens was split equally between the army, the canteen steward and the NCOs.

On the same day they decided to let the Rose & Crown, Sutton on the Forest, to William Pearce, a farmer from Somerset, who had come to York the previous October. He had a deposit of £200 with the National Provincial Bank and they felt that for that reason alone he would make them a very suitable tenant.

1 July 1884

Barwick, of the White Swan, Goodramgate, York, came in with his wife to see them about his poor trading position. They considered him a foolish man and reckless about money matters; although his takings were good at £20 a week, he had bought 'household goods' and ought to be watched. They gave him back his £50 deposit paid on entry against his promise to pay his monthly trading account as it fell due. They spelled it out for him, and perhaps for themselves, as it was entered in the diary 'goods supplied by 11 June to be paid for by 11 July – and so on'. However, in such mercantile matters they had neither Tetley's resolution nor Tetley's product.

Pearce, the acceptable face of tenancy, came in and confessed. He was not called Pearce, his real name was Digth (*sic*). He had left Yeovil in order to be lost to his family. Enquiries to the police revealed no wrongdoing on his part and he was allowed to apply for the transfer of the licence into his name.

2 July 1884

The firm advertised its haymaking and harvesting of ales in the *York Herald*. Supplying those who helped to get in the hay and the corn with beer was a tradition of farming life, absolutely obeyed; they were thin beers, designed to slacken thirst rather than inebriate. They usually came in small casks of some four gallons, which were dumped in the nearest stream to keep cool and drawn upon at set times throughout the day. The beer was drunk from mugs fashioned from bovine horns, resistant to rough usage; also, they would only hold half a pint at a time. At a time of intensive manual labour, this was useful trade to obtain.

This day contained an entry on the progress of the rights of the Strensall Common Right Holders; Wilkinson, the solicitor, had been to London and appeared before a select committee of the House of Commons, which had ordered the War Office to pay all the costs of the 1877–80 Strensall bill and £100 towards the present costs. He reported that the assessment of the value of the common right holders would be dealt with by the Land Clauses Act, and this would be all the better for the holders. Wilkinson expressed himself disgusted with Melrose, who had apparently done his best for the opposition in crying down that value – and this when it should be realized that he had sold the firm two houses in Strensall. The partners were apoplectic.

5 July 1884

They dealt with the domestic problem of their caretaker/housekeeper at the George Street offices. They were going to engage Mrs Baker, offering her five shillings a week and rent-free living accommodation with a coal and gas allowance. Mrs Blakey was to have ten shillings a week pension and to leave (they noted in the diary 'to go away'). They were relieved to have solved the matter, piously noting it was worth it for an extra three shillings a week and, what was more, it was a good bargain, for they would have somebody clean about the place. What is interesting is the payment of a pension to her; her long service and their sense of *noblesse oblige* denoted the duty they felt.

9 July 1884

They got their gas bill for the six months to the end of June for the Tadcaster brewery. It was for £41 10s 6d, being 151,000 cubic feet at 5s 6d per 1000 feet. The response was visceral and automatic — 'it was frightful in amount and wasteful in use and something had to be done about it.' A calculation showed that annually they would be spending about £100 a year for lighting at the brewery.

10 July 1884

Lord Wenlock was understood to have been very satisfied on the way Horsley (a brewery tenant) had managed the book at Crocky Hill, and wanted him to do the agricultural show at Escrick on the following Wednesday. Horsley had declined to do it because it was Fair Day, and he only had the 'decency' (heavy sarcasm) to mention this to the partners the previous day. They cajoled him into doing it, but he played hard to get, for he said he could not do it because he had nothing in which to cook peas and potatoes; so they took him to Lamberts, who had nothing suitable and then on to Hill's, who had just the right equipment. They recorded that tenants just had 'no push' in them, but failed to notice that this one had just the 'push' needed to get what he wanted.

11 July 1884

A heavy storm had broken over York and the partners were busy writing out a list of houses in which either the roofs had given way or the drains had blocked; there were eight properties affected.

On the same day they agreed to buy from Kilvington, the builder, a plot of land in Leeman Road, York, for £120. He was to do the necessary paving, lay the drains and make the road. If they could get a licence they felt they would do a good trade, for 100 houses had already been built there and 500 more were planned. The site was close to the iron foundry and to the workshops of the North Eastern Railway Company. There was no other public house supplying beer or wine for three-quarters of a mile, so in their opinion it would be a capital house. They calculated their investment as land £120, building £350, fittings £80 and extras £50 – total £600. They could let the house for £330 a year. Their assessment of the proposition, a mixture of unarticulated experience and cautious optimism, prevails to this day in brewery thinking, the only difference being that pages and pages are covered with pseudo-scientific analysis in justification, with all sides of the proposition considered to distraction, time lost and caveats inserted by ambitious company men anxious not to be committed in the event of failure. The partners prepared a petition to circulate to householders in the area, soliciting their support for a licence application to be made on 25 August. They confirmed their earlier decision to apply for a removal of the licence of the Sun, Tanner Row.

They learned that Mitchell Brothers of Castleford, brewers and public-house owners in liquidation, had not yet disposed of their tied properties. They wrote to the agents for further information and were told that the houses were bringing in about £5000 a year, that the asking price was £14,000 and that the rent roll was £700 a year. They wanted more information and if they got it would think about negotiating.

14 July 1884

There was still trouble on the domestic front. Having thought that Mrs Baker would take over George Street, they got back word that she would come only if the firm would allow her to have lodgers; a firm refusal was given to this. Smelly Mrs Blakey remained in office.

17 July 1884

Parker waxed indignant about an order being placed with Osborne & Scott for wine. He remonstrated that Young & Company of Liverpool had always supplied Tarragona satisfactorily and it was most undesirable that any new firm should be brought in. This provoked a series of diary entries of some warmth, that Young & Company's last delivery had been thick and bad, with an unpleasant palate, and that was the reason for the change of supplier.

23 July 1884

Parker had a long interview with Colonel Phillips of the 20th Husssars and got nowhere in his efforts to secure the right to supply the canteen. The colonel admitted that the Manchester beer was not all it could be, but he had received no complaints about it from the canteen sergeant or the men and, in any case, he felt that the beer sold at the Barrack Tavern was 'most moderate stuff', and it only sold because that house was the last one before the barracks. Parker was stunned into silence.

24 July 1884

Mrs Kilvington reported to the partners that she had an excellent woman to replace the fragrant Mrs Blakey. She was a daughter of the founder of the *Yorkshire Gazette* no less, about 50 years old and currently engaged in looking after clergymen's houses when they left town. She promised to send her round for inspection with the recommendation that she was an excellent cook as well. The partners saw her the next day. Her name was Mrs Smith, of Hill's Court, Lord Mayor's Walk, and she was a widow. She told them about her previous appointments and said that she would require 12 shillings a week and a girl to help her. Parker's enthusiasm was controlled – he said he would let her know.

28 July 1884

Parker heard a rumour that the 3rd Hussars were coming from Hounslow; he was not disheartened by Colonel Phillips's put-down, and hastened to write to him to ask for a good word to be put in for the firm with regard to the supply of beer. Meantime, the tenant of the Barrack Tavern came into the office to say that unless he served the soldiers returning to the barracks with the weakest beer, they would never get back! A touching solicitude conveniently harnessed to commercial advantage.

29 July 1884

Mrs Blakey's problem continued; she promised to try to keep things cleaner, and said that when her daughter married towards the end of the year she would go and live with her. The partners reconsidered her proposed pension and reduced the figure to 5s a week as being appropriate to the changed circumstances.

They kept up the pressure to get the barracks trade; Colonel Phillips unexpectedly called into the office the following day to try the beer, but the partners had no sample for tasting; it had gone to complete an order from the North Riding Asylum. This was explained to the colonel who went away very unimpressed.

The next day they went up to the barracks to inspect the canteen cellars; unfortunately, Brett of Manchester was there. The partners thought he was very sour; for good measure, they thought the same about his beer. On the same day a section of lead guttering on the Angel, Walmgate, fell into the street; luckily, they recorded in the diary, no one was injured. They went over to the barracks again and saw Flint, the canteen steward, who said the partners' beer did not compare with Brett's, but when they pointed out that it was the beer Colonel Phillips wanted, Flint gave up his objection and became 'very civil'.

31 July 1884

Parker called on Captain Thurston at Strensall camp, and obtained another order for beer. He discovered that the canteen seemed very pleased with the XXX (best mild).

On the same day he went over to Tadcaster and spoke to Caswell, the head brewer, and complained bitterly about the dirtiness of the place. He tested the yeast, which he considered very good but too dark, so perhaps a change was needed. Some of the wooden tubs were leaking and he advised they should be caulked with oakum and then painted.

Somewhere in his travels he saw Rennison, who owed back rent to the brewery and who promised to pay something on account when he had sold his potatoes.

1 August 1884

Parker went to Leeds and saw Messrs Beevers & Spice about Mitchell Brothers of Castleford. He was told that the committee had not discussed whether they would sell the houses away from the brewery. However, some prospective buyers from London had been given until the next day to make up their minds, failing which the partners would get a chance. There were nine fully licensed houses, six beer houses and sixteen cottages, all let at a total rent of £685 annually. Arrangements were made for the partners to be in Castleford the following Tuesday to look round the property. The trade was estimated at £5000 a year in beer and stout, and there was no tie for spirits. Parker thought the proposition well worth consideration, subject to inspection and the state of the properties. Later in the day they fell out among themselves about being out of stock and about the discounts the firm was offering. They all had different ideas about how much stock they had in hand.

5 August 1884

Parker had a friend into the office and offered him a glass of beer, which the friend found undrinkable. This led to a series of vivid entries in the diary and a complete departure from the original topic. The day's entries wound up with a discussion about the proposed transfer of a beer house licence, which had turned out to be a full licence. The final note said 'Will partners check their facts before making entries'.

6 August 1884

They went over to Castleford and saw Mitchell's brewery; they thought that the beer was frightful and that they could do very well with their own beer. They visited some of Mitchell's houses and resolved to see the rest before deciding what to do.

Colonel Phillips came in from the barracks and complained about the beer being sent there; the partners were angry and felt insulted. Poole Senior told them he was willing to be their agent, but not at the commission they were offering. Later in the day they went up to the barracks to see the colonel again. They told him the beer was excellent, but got the riposte that it was highly coloured and tasted peculiar. They came away feeling there was a great prejudice against them.

7 August 1884

They went over to Castleford and offered to buy ten of Mitchell's houses for £6400; the diary set out the details of their calculations on price and trade, with notes about nearby competition from free houses. The next day Beevers said it would take £8000 for the houses and brewery, so they offered this and became the owners of the Whitwood Mere Brewery, Castleford.

11 August 1884

They wrote to Poole Senior offering him a position as a traveller and devoted some space in the diary to justifying how they could afford to pay the salary and commission.

They then went off for their summer holidays – Dundas to Welwood, Muirkirk, Ayrshire, and then on to Ardgowan, Greenock; and Parker to Harsley Hall, Northallerton.

14 August 1884

The occupants of the North Eastern Hotel wrote in to complain about the great noise Mrs Lund of the Grapes was making with her piano; the partners *en masse* promised to call in and see her about this. The properties adjoined in Tanner Row.

15 August 1884

Parker went over to Alne to listen to complaints about Tose, the tenant of their public house there, who was alleged to be permanently drunk. He enquired of the vicar, the village shopkeeper and the village constable, all of whom said that while he used to drink, he had calmed down. Overnight the vicar had second thoughts, so wrote to Parker to say that he thought that Tose was in fact unfit to be the tenant of a public house. He was given notice.

The partners renewed their assault on the barracks for business. A softly, softly approach was decided on – they carried out a programme of visits to army units and were gratified to learn that Colonel Phillips proposed writing to his opposite number in the 3rd Hussars and to Major Balders, formerly of the 5th Dragoons, to recommend their beer.

18 August 1884

Tose was removed from the Blue Bell, and the village constable appointed tenant!

19 August 1884

They were invited to supply the bars for the Conservative Party picnic at Hovingham and got their catering tenant, Horsley, to do it for them. However, trade turned out 'wretched', for they sold only one and a half barrels and one kilderkin of stout because all the people who attended listened to the speeches and had no time to drink. They were very put out about this.

5 September 1884

They formally took over Mitchell's brewery and houses. They decided to visit all the houses and sign the tenants up on new tenancy agreements.

They discussed whether to buy an oil gas machine for £142; it was designed to manufacture gas on the premises for between 50 and 60 lights. Presumably, this installation was intended for the brewery.

6 September 1884

Someone complained in the diary that the *Contract Book* could not be found; there was an immediate response — 'somebody had not bothered to look on the window ledge behind the blind'. This led to a silence, for no entries appeared for several days.

12 September 1884

An analysis was done of the gross profit margin on own brewed beers. They calculated the gross value of racked beer (that is, beer ready for sale) and the price fetched for grains sold at £2975 16s 3d. The gross cost of production for malt, hops, sugar and duty was £1362 15s 3d, so they were left with a gross profit of £1613 1s 0d on the month's brewing – 54.25 per cent – their combined mathematics were holding up. The average price of hops was 1s 4¼d and duty was 24s 7s 5d per quarter; they had used 342½ quarters of malt and 36 cwts of sugar. The gross profit had fallen by 0.75 per cent on July and, in their estimation, this was due to there being too few Treble X and bitter brews in the month, and also to fewer extracts because of the quantity of Smyrna malt used; barley at 29s could not be expected to yield the same amount of extract as Yorkshire barley at 34s 6d did. The conclusion (clear to the diarist, if not to the reader) was that if they changed to Smyrna barley at 40 shillings they would gain in malting what they lost in brewing.

Having done this calculation for the benefit of the rest to digest at their leisure, the partner went off to the barracks to see Captain Thurston, who told him that the Treble X was the best beer the brewery had yet sent out and was much liked, so he ordered another six hogsheads. He also received payment for the July and August accounts, so the day ended well – well, not quite, because he went to see Air, the tenant of the Ship Inn, York, who owed £100 8s 6d on his valuation. Air declared it was not worth a penny except as firewood, so they went through it together and agreed on £70. Air then stated he wanted to be 'secured' against the £70 in the event of the brewery failing financially. The partner was outraged at the statement and declared that Air was the first person who had ever distrusted the firm and that he would have to think whether Air could remain as tenant after such an insult.

He then went round to Mr Phillips, a solicitor, and asked him if he could induce his client, Mrs Wilson, to reduce the rent the firm was paying for the Nag's Head, Heworth. Phillips said he would see what could be done.

13 September 1884

There was a visit to the brewery; the fermentation was considered very good and the new Burton yeast was felt to be responsible. It was noted that the steam copper leaked badly and that Tindall, the engineer, had said that he would have to get a Leeds firm to deal with it in a day. Lord Neville's hops were thought to be very good and cheap as well, at £6.

Pasted into the diary was a cutting from the *Yorkshire Post* about the takeover of Mitchell's brewery containing the following: 'Castleford is a large district and no doubt the inhabitants will appreciate the splendid ales etc. that the Tadcaster Brewery Company are so noted for supplying.' In very small print indeed is a statement that this was an advertisement.

One of the partners made a note in the diary that he was going over to Scarborough to stay with Mr C. H. Tripp, at 4 St Nicholas Parade. Tripp later became general manager of the company from 1887 to 1894.

Monro put in a note that any letters for him were to be opened by the other partners and then sent on to 32 Curzon Street, London. Dawnay went on holiday on 15 September and left his address as Tor Castle, Banaire, Fort William, North Britain – a common usage for Scotland to emphasize the unity of the two countries. Newton complained that his sherry was bad and he would return it.

Later in September a note appeared that Welsh wished to take the tenancy of the Wheatsheaf, Hungate, York, and was prepared to pay £20 down on the valuation and £1 a month until paid off. Then followed an entry to the effect that 'if Welsh is the same chap that held the Phoenix, then he still owed £65 to the firm, and he is not a fit person to have confidence in.'

24 September 1884

An entry about the proposed gas installation at Tadcaster; the partners felt that if Rogers Brothers were prepared to maintain it to their satisfaction for three years free of charge, then the firm would buy it. Alternatively, if the installation was made and payment for it was deferred for six months, then if it proved satisfactory and the gas consumed came to under 2s 6d per 1000 square (*sic*) feet, as stated by them, they would buy it. Otherwise, it would have to be removed.

Rogers replied that they did not agree to this and that anyway the gas would cost 10 shillings per 1000 square feet, which left the partners in a rage (it must have done, for they repeated the square feet mistake), and they said they would not purchase the apparatus at any price.

25 September 1884

A partner went over to Castleford to see how matters were progressing and was satisfied with the sales; he returned via Leeds, where he stopped off to chase up some accounts.

26 September 1884

The great gas affair continued. Parker was at the brewery and saw the local manager of the gas company, and told him that unless there was a reduction in price, they would install their own apparatus. He received the reply that the only person who could authorize a reduction was the secretary of the company at Wetherby. It was suggested that Parker write to the chairman of the company, Mr W. Huggan of Pudsey. He learned that John Smith's brewery, together with several other Tadcaster businesses, had cut off the gas, and Ingleby, the miller, was having electric lights put in.

Old Mr Hotham called in at the offices and collected his rent of £1565 5s 9d due to 1 January 1884. While the partners were concerned about prompt payment by their debtors, they did not seem to apply the same conscientious thought to their own payments. Most of the partners' daily routine consisted of chasing money from tenants and agents and finding tenants for their houses.

The gas supply at the brewery continued to exercise them. The evenings were drawing in and a decision had to be made. They reconnected the gas supply from the gas company after three months with a severe warning to the brewer to use it carefully. Rogers's apparatus was not considered as cheap as first thought and the refusal of any guarantee by that firm rankled. However, they were asked to meet the partners at the brewers' show in London to discuss the whole matter and to see if an understanding could be reached.

1 October 1884

It was noted that beer sales for September were 50,285 gallons against 38,095 for the same month the previous year. A careful stock of all malt, beer, wines and spirits and other sundries at Tadcaster and Castleford was taken after all employees had left the premises.

They thought about borrowing £6000 at 4 per cent, but the solicitor for the lender stated that he would not lend the money for ten years, but only so long as the lender remained alive. This confounded the partners and they determined to ascertain who the lender was and how old he was. They stocked up with dispense vessels, ordering from the Barker Pottery Company of Chesterfield, 50 half-gallon, 100 one-gallon, 200 two-gallon and 150 four-gallon jugs, all to be stamped 'TADCASTER TOWER BREWERY COMPANY, GEORGE STREET, YORK'.

In October, no doubt influenced by the short days and long dark nights, the partners considered prospective tenants; none had any money. Mr Petts, of the Londesbrough, York, complained that while he was living, he was not putting anything by; the comment was that he should be very lucky for he was holding his own.

For the 12 months to 30 September the firm sold 513,505 gallons at a total value of £29,263; the figures for the previous year were 400,204 gallons and £23,489. Sales of wines and spirits were 14,921 gallons at £11,723; the previous year it had been 15,380 and £12,152.

They received a letter from Lord Neville about the price of hops, saying that it should be about £5 10s per cwt, and in the same letter he forgot this and stated that he had sold some on the previous day at £5 5s.

5 October 1884

The partners learned that the unknown lender of money was Mr Ford's mother, of the law firm of Ford & Warren of Leeds. Since on her death her money would pass to Mr Ford, there was little risk of it being called in. Beevers, the Leeds' valuer, had found this source for them (apparently in connection with the Mitchell purchase) at a good rate of interest, and then they disputed with him his fee for doing so. They decided to sleep on the matter before making a decision whether to pay him.

On the same day one of the draymen, Parkin, who had been instructed to go to the Rose & Crown, Sutton on the Forest, with a mare and light cart, failed to return on time. Apparently he had gone to Sutton on Derwent in error or forgetfulness, and had tried to get to Sutton on the Forest by way of Strensall, along Sandy

Lane, a very indifferent road. The mare became exhausted, fell down and the shafts of the cart were broken, and Parkin left stranded. He carried the delivery of spirits to his destination and stayed the night at Sutton on the Forest.

9 October 1884

The big bay horse had been very ill during the night and the partners came to the conclusion that, since the veterinary surgeon had been up all night with the animal and the cost was enormous, it was time the horse went. They went through the past year's accounts and found that the vet had spent most of his time with this one horse. The next day one of the town horses was taken ill with a chill, but recovered. Parker would no doubt, in the full course of his brewery career, at some time appreciate there was something to be said for motor vehicles as brewery transport.

It was not a good time; the coming winter days brought their woes. Dixon, who looked after the public houses as an outdoor inspector, was not doing well at all; he was lazy and untidy. He was given a severe dressing down and told that if he did not alter his ways considerably, a change would be made. At the Three Cranes, Lendal, York, the ousted tenant, Saul, refused to leave and the person sent to replace him was bodily thrown out by Saul's friends into the street. Eventually he did go and the partners recorded that the Saul family were a thoroughly bad lot. Harland, a traveller, was allowed to drive the freshly clipped pony on the previous Saturday round the Strensall area; in turning a corner, he managed to break one of the cart shafts. The partners were so incensed that they insisted he paid for the repair, believing he had been careless. However, they also decided to have the pony shod, so perhaps it was not entirely his fault.

22 October 1884

They went to Middlesbrough to look at Robinson's (129 Newport Road), doing 12 hogsheads a week. It was on offer to them to buy; they had been told there were several off-licence shops in Newport Road, two of which were doing 50 hogsheads between them, as there were 15,000 people living in the vicinity and restrictive covenants against any other licensed premises. The vendor produced his receipts and invoices, and they noted that most of the beer was from Charrington's. The price required was £1200 for the house plus £100 for the valuation. They left to go back to York and on the way did their calculations on what they could afford to pay and how much profit they could make. Then there was a hint of caution – were they being told the whole truth? They recovered their confidence and felt it was a very desirable house to acquire; even better to manage if only they could find an honest manager! Middlesbrough was a boom town in the 1880s, expanding like an American immigrant town, with plenty of spending money and a profligate attitude. It was a time too when the London brewers, Charrington's, were in expansionist mood.

25 October 1884

The partners were in London and hoped to see Rogers about the gas supply problem, but he did not turn up, so they decided to abandon the scheme to go ahead with their own manufacture, and continue with the gas company. They compromised by promising themselves to consume less gas in the winter, and none at all in the summer – a vain hope.

28 October 1884

One of the partners, unidentifiable from the handwriting and therefore not often in the office, felt it his duty on a rare visit to enter an indignant note that Dixon, the stableman, was giving cold instead of chilled water to the horses and was standing around with his coat on doing nothing when he could have usefully employed his time in cleaning out. He demanded a change. The following day Dixon got his marching orders – a week's notice because he was lazy, untidy and dirty.

The partners made further enquiries about the desirable public house in Middlesbrough. They found that another house nearby was about to be altered and improved and that it would take away all Robinson's trade. What was more to the point, the existing trade of Robinson's was obtained by the licensee giving double measure to the customers; he had bought the house for £600 and was doing the classic trick of working up the trade, exciting eager brewers and selling quickly. They noted again that he had only paid £600 for the property. They wrote their views in the diary with the righteous wrath of men who had uncovered a scandal, with not one word about their former enthusiasm. They resolved to have nothing further to do with the proposition.

The surveyor of taxes wrote to say that he wanted to see Monro about income tax. He was told that Monro was in France but that those who were in York would answer any questions they could in his absence.

1 November 1884

They wrote to Melrose asking for a reduction in the rent they paid for the Ebor, Marcia and Rose & Crown public houses; they had calculated they had lost £100 a year on having them.

6 November 1884

Melrose called in to the office and, after a great deal of pressing by them, agreed to reduce the rent from £150 to £110 yearly. The partners felt pleased with themselves and their negotiating skills and said so.

It was an eventful day for the partnership; Frederick William Browne, an original partner from 1875, retired from the partnership, leaving Thomas Newton (who had tagged on to his name Russell), Henry Monro, Sir Frederick George Milner (who had succeeded to the baronetcy), the Honourable Reginald Parker and the Honourable Geoffrey Nicholas Dawnay to sail the ship of commerce. They were upset at the way the *York Herald* handled the news. It missed the point entirely that Browne was retiring and implied that the partnership was being dissolved. They called upon their solicitor to discuss the matter. He said there was nothing wrong with the announcement as printed and published. They were far from satisfied, no doubt led on by Monro, so they tackled Hargreaves, the *York Herald*'s publisher, and he obscurely blamed his London correspondent. However, he apologized and the *York Herald* published a detailed statement correcting any misunderstanding.

A new groom for the horses was appointed to replace the scruffy Dixon; he was Charles Durham of Thorganby, a farmer's son, strong and steady — they felt.

7 November 1884

The surveyor of taxes called in person at the office and wanted to know why the partners had returned an income tax statement for the year ended April 1885 at £4438, compared to £5765 for the previous year. They explained that times were hard and he agreed to let it stand, so with tax at 5d in the pound, the levy was £92 10s.

They noted it was less than they had paid the previous year, but – a thought struck them – only if Gladstone did not put up the tax to pay for the troubles in the Sudan. The partners did not view either Gladstone's or General Gordon's efforts on behalf of the Empire and Egypt with any enthusiasm, if it meant paying for the honour.

A few days later Mr Hotham came in for his rent. Paying rent depressed them and it was always reflected in the tone of the diary entries for some days afterwards. As if that depression was not enough, the solicitors, Ford & Warren, indicated that they were not prepared to lend the firm the £6000 promised through Beevers; the reason given was that the security offered was mainly licensed premises.

They tackled Beevers, who said that they had supplied all the necessary information and that they thought Ford & Warren were not giving the real truth about their refusal. The Leeds traveller told them that there was a general outcry in Leeds about the state of the trade and that his customers had told him that they had never known things so quiet and so bad.

17 November 1884

The diary recorded the largest sale of beer the firm had ever made – 190 barrels. It was written down without comment. The collective depression still persisted; so they looked at the various travellers' sales efforts. Poole was taken to task and the suggestion made to him that he should take £50 less salary and 6d a barrel less commission; things were bad, for Poole said he would consider the matter and let them know. Green was told that unless he did 20 barrels in weekly sales, it would be of no use and he would not be kept. He protested, but was plainly told what they thought of his (in)activity.

28 November 1884

Altoft Cooperative Society asked for a quotation for the supply of spirits and was given the following: 'Delivered to Normanton railway station – Jamaica rum 16s per gallon proof; pale brandy 21s; best pale brandy 25s; best old brown brandy 30s; Nicholson's gin 12s; port and sherry 10s.'

A notice was sent to Marshall, the tenant of the Duke's Head, York, that they had received reports that he made customers drunk on Sunday mornings, and to the tenant of the Punchbowl, also in York, that he was rather slack about his closing times. It might be wondered if Marshall had the liberty to intoxicate his customers after midday on Sunday and quite what the reasons were for the inebriety on Sunday mornings – perhaps the sermons drove them to the drink or intoxication before morning service removed the need to attend. Poole's services were dispensed with; he was given a testimonial.

Just before Christmas the partners were at Castleford and the vicar, the Reverend J. J. Needham, learning of their coming, called on them to ask what the firm would give towards his new chapel, and annually for local charities.

Astutely, he promised his ale account would be placed with the firm after Christmas; he was paid in his own coin – the partners replied that they would think about the matter after Christmas. They did in fact decide to give two guineas to the chapel and three guineas for the charities, with the hope to be able to do this every year.

Just before the holiday Parker went down to the family home at Shirburn Castle, Tetsworth, Oxfordshire, for some rest. He had undoubtedly worried and striven for the partnership through some difficult months and deserved it.

After the holiday period the problems began again. Poole's father wrote insulting letters to the firm about his son having to leave. The partners found out that while Poole Junior had been paid by customers for supplies, he had not handed over the money to the brewery; there was great consternation.

Green, who had taken a reduction in salary and commission, still could not make his job pay, for the partners lost £46 18s 6d on the trading account from October to January. So they reduced his salary from £200 to £100, with the declaration that if he did not accept, then he would have to leave their employ.

There now occurred a gap of some four years in the diary, in all probability not because the diary was not kept, but because the volumes have been lost. The problems remain the same when it resumes in 1888.

3
Consolidation, 1888

In January Kendall, tenant of the Cross Keys, Dunnington, was rumoured to be buying his beer from Turner of Gate Helmsley and his spirits from Sellers of York, quite contrary to the tie — a cardinal sin in the brewer's book. Employees were sent to search the house and Kendall given notice to leave on the grounds that even if the rumour were false, he had not been paying his trade account on time, and he and his wife drank heavily. The search revealed no damning evidence, but the notice stayed.

26 January 1888

The Old George Hotel in York was sold at auction and bought by the sitting tenant for £4080. The partners noted that really good houses in York still kept their price.

They were pleased to note that most of the regiments coming to the camp at Strensall during the year were on their list and greatly in excess of the previous year; the assessment of the situation cheered them up.

27 January 1888

They observed their own bottled beer threw a heavy deposit, and resolved in future to bottle only Guinness stout and Bass ale in order to restore their customers' confidence in their bottled beers.

30 January 1888

Mr Wray, a solicitor from Hull, called upon them in the office at

York and told them that he had the 'throating' of the Hull brewers, Gleadow Dibb & Company, and was anxious to do the same for the partners. There was no comment by the partners on this entry, but it would appear he was saying that he had an advantage that could be exploited.

31 January 1888

The cold weather must have made them peevish; they issued instructions that the unbusinesslike and very undesirable practice of clerks in the firm's various offices of writing to one another on ordinary business matters must stop. They quoted an example – Holden of the Grimsby office wrote a private letter to Buchanan in the York office about ordering gantries and acknowledging an order sent to Grimsby. The manager was requested to give notice to all clerks in their employ, including the brewer, that all letters having reference to the firm's business should be addressed to 'The Manager, Tower Brewery, Grimsby, York, Castleford etc etc'.

The Grimsby office and depot had not long been opened, and perhaps the informal commercial ways of Lincolnshire were in danger of spreading across the Humber, and had to be stopped. The diary recorded a remark by one of the partners that the hock from Grimsby at 30s was not worth 18s, that the sherry was poor and that he hoped the port would be better value. Another partner replied that they had been obliged to take the Grimsby wines at valuation and it was a pity they did not please. The traditional solution was proposed, namely to blend off the unacceptable wines with new stock.

4 February 1888

One of them was doing the rounds of the headquarters of the regiments intending to have their summer camps at Strensall; he reported on his visits to Hounslow and Hampton Court, interviewing Major Ward and the sergeants. He agreed prices for beers, wines, spirits and soft drinks; he was sufficiently pleased on the discounts he gave to write that he considered they were good prices. He then went on to the hop merchants and bought a considerable quantity, enough to last them 12 months, noting that the hop merchant he had dealt with had made a large sale to

Bass – £14,000. It could only have been Monro who did these visits – it was his style of reporting.

Dawson, tenant of the Crown in York at £80 annual rent, was found to be subletting the billiard room and one other room for £62; they were much put out by the news.

9 February 1888

Maule, the brewer, was discovered to be using maize malt without telling anybody; he was reprimanded and the diary noted that the ticking off would keep him in his place in future.

13 February 1888

The partners received two recommendations for requests for tenancies (1) from Colonel Legg for his servant Thomas Pollard, who had £60 to pay for the valuation, and (2) from Prince Albert Victor (the Duke of Clarence and then a captain in that regiment) for Sergeant Major Culham of B Troop 9th Lancers. Culham was immediately given the Leopard, York.

Dundas, brother of the Marquis of Zetland, who had been admitted as a partner in 1887, had still not paid his contribution into the firm's reserves, and there were several entries by the others in the diary drawing his attention to this omission. He was shamed into paying up on 15 February.

18 February 1888

The lease by which they held their houses from Hotham was got out and examined, and the opinion of Badger, the solicitor, obtained. Sadly, they decided that it was a full repairing lease by the firm and that the stable at the White Swan, Goodramgate, York, which had blown down, must be restored at their cost. They felt this was very hard; it must have been serious for them, for they discussed it on a Saturday in the hunting season.

The telephone company applied to put telephone poles through some of the firm's properties; the application was ignored for the time being. The traveller covering Beverley complained that his district was not worth working and that it was a failure. They came to the conclusion that as he had a fair writing hand and had worked in a bank, they would bring him into the office as a clerk at 21 shillings a week on trial, and get rid of Lofthouse, who was highly unsatisfactory.

Durham came into the office and complained strongly about the new bay horse, which had nearly killed him, and he absolutely refused to take it out again. The horse was handed over to Marshall to see if he could do any better.

24 February 1888

There was a note that in the previous year they sold no less than 50,726 gallons of ale and stout to the army canteens at Strensall.

Burke, tenant of the Spread Eagle, York, said he was going up to Tyneside where he had many friends and would see what he could do about getting some business for the firm. They therefore gave him some cards and asked him to distribute them.

5 March 1888

Durham was sacked for being drunk. He was given one week's notice and left immediately. They commented that he had never seemed to value his place.

7 March 1888

The young bay horse was behaving much better and was quieter with Marshall; with plenty of work, they felt he would make a good horse yet.

10 March 1888

One of the partners went to Newark from York by train to see the sergeant major of the Derby militia about getting the canteen supplies when they came to Strensall for their summer camp. He reported that he was hopeful the firm would get the order. He noted that he left York at 12.45 p.m. and got back at 8.00 p.m.

On the same day there is an entry that T. Newton was publicly examined about his financial affairs; apparently he had gone bankrupt.

14 March 1888

There was a note that there had been heavy falls of snow and that the intense cold had 'quietened the beer trade very much, but that on the other hand the spirit trade had gone up'. It was an ill wind.

15 March 1888

There was a frenzy of disparate entries; one to the effect that *The Times* newspaper should be ordered for the following Tuesday to find out about the proposals for local government reform (which became the Local Government Act of 1888 and which transferred many powers from the justices to newly created county councils and county boroughs); another was insistent that cover should be provided for the beer drays which stood out in all weather and were being ruined; and a third that the Castleford horses were not being fed enough and that samples of their feed should be sent for and examined. Indeed, beware the Ides.

16 March 1888

One of the partners went over to Grimsby to see how matters stood in the new outpost of the firm. He returned after a long day and a cold journey. He recorded this fact for the benefit of those choosing to stay at home and went on to voice his concern at the fall in trade. He recommended that an old man employed at 24 shillings a week was of no real value and could easily be replaced by a strong lad at 10s. Holden, the office manager, took up the suggestion with enthusiasm and got rid of an office lad at 15s a week and replaced him with a good one at 5s. All good work, one might think, but would it have been done without the visit by a partner to stir matters? It was an overnight stay and the partner put in a lot of visits to houses. He left Grimsby at 4.50 p.m., stopping off *en route* back to York, eventually getting there at 7.40 p.m. The partners rather liked recording times precisely where they could; it was the measure of their activity to the others.

19 March 1888

It was noted that the weather continued very severe and cold, the snow stopping all trade. It was also noted that there had been an outbreak of smallpox at Grimsby, which was so bad that victims were being carried in a black van to the hospital at the rate of six or seven a day.

20 March 1888

They were very concerned about the contents of the Local Government Bill, which had just been published. The items that disturbed them most were proposals to introduce compensation for the non-renewal of a freehold public-house licence and to increase the annual licence duty. The Yorkshire Brewers' Association had a meeting about the bill in Leeds, which they attended.

27 March 1888

Maule, the brewer, requested that a telephone be installed in his house – the cost was £5. The partners were happy to comply with the request and told him that he could pay for it.

On the same day the budget proposals were published. There was no increase in beer duty, but there was a tax of 5s for every dozen bottles of champagne and imported wines. There was also a tax on drays and carts. The good news was that the budget surplus had brought a 1d reduction in income tax, so it would be 6d in the pound when they paid their dues the following January.

9 April 1888

Monro went off to London for a short holiday; Dundas went abroad – to the Hotel Mont Fleurie, Cannes.

Those left at home fell out about feeding the horses; a note stated that the horses were getting wretched oats and that good oats were cheaper than the rate they were paying for bad oats. Furthermore, the hay was mouldy and everybody knew that horses were more delicate in the spring than at any other time of the year and that bad feed affected their kidneys. Another remarked that nothing on their public house at Heslington showed that it belonged to the firm: '*no doubt* the preparation of a signboard was in hand.'

14 April 1888

Spring was in the air and they felt cheerful. They noted that malting was going very well, and another month would see them through and some six weeks earlier than the previous year. There was no sign of mould on the steeping floors of the malting and they had never had a better season.

But the brewing industry was working itself into a high state of concern about the Local Government Bill and the power given therein for justices to refuse the renewal of licences. All the country brewers were to meet in London later in the month.

First, the good news from Burke, their agent on Tyneside, that the beer was selling well in Jarrow – in fact it was the best beer in the district.

Then the bad news; the sergeant major of the Leicester Yeomanry wrote to say he had made messing arrangements elsewhere. They told one another that it was no use writing letters; people like sergeant majors needed to be made a fuss over and called upon in person. Too true.

A note in the diary records their views about opening an agency for the Spalding area of Lincolnshire; they were thorough, as they had reconnoitred the ground and taken opinions on trade prospects.

21 April 1888

They decided to give white maize malt a trial; the reason being it cost 26s 3d a quarter, with an extract yield of 100 lbs. Barley malt yielded an extract of 88 lbs, and cost 36 shillings a quarter. So much for telling off Maule, the brewer, for using maize without prior consent; they were converted to the idea by the saving.

* * *

11 May 1888

It was noted in the diary that the telephone had been installed and was in working order. Drawn like children to the novelty, they lost no time in using their new acquisition. A note in the diary the following day recorded its first use – no doubt to the discomfiture of the recipient of the call, who was accustomed to being left on his own and to knowing (from travel routines and a knowledge of the railway timetable between York and Tadcaster) when his masters were likely to descend on him. They telephoned Maule at the brewery and were to the point. How many spent grains were left over from brewing and what steps was he taking

Nun Appleton Hall, near Tadcaster, birthplace of Sir Frederick Milner, one of the partners in the brewery.

York. Davygate.

C.J. MELROSE & CO
WINE AND SPIRIT IMPORTERS

ABOVE. Davygate, a principal shopping street in the city centre connecting St Sampson's and Helen's Squares.

BELOW. St Sampson's Square at the turn of the century.

St. Sampson's Square, York.

SHEPHERD'S CITY BATHS
TURKISH BATHS
SLIPPER BATHS
H. WARD

ABOVE. A view of Coney Street, an ancient city thoroughfare parallel to the river Ouse.

BELOW. Walmgate Bar at the turn of the century.

A watercolour showing Lendal Bridge and the magnificent Victorian Gothic pile of the Yorkshire Club.

A lithograph by F. Bedford junior, of the 1840s, showing one of the three Water Lanes which sloped down from Nessgate to the King's Staith, next to the Ouse Bridge.

C. ABBOTT

(Late "SCAWIN"),

RAIL WAY AND FAMILY HOTEL,

(FIRST CLASS)

YORK.

Established many years. Refurnished and thoroughly renovated. Adjoining the Station Gates. The largest Hotel in York. Private Rooms. Ladies' and Gentlemen's Coffee Rooms. Every accommodation for Night Travellers. Porters attend the Station night and day. A good commercial connection attached to this house. Excellent Stabling. Brilliant Saloon.

N.B.—ASK FOR ABBOTT'S PORTERS.

YORK.

BLACK SWAN HOTEL,

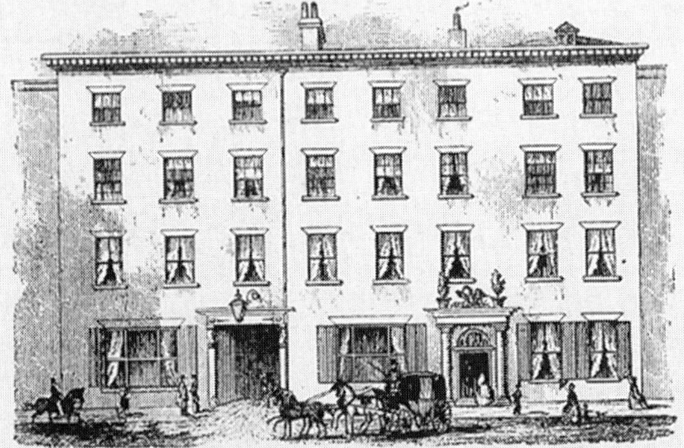

CONEY STREET.

This is the only exclusively *Family Hotel*, centrally situated, Winn's "George Hotel" having been pulled down.

This old-established COUNTY HOTEL has been entirely renovated and newly furnished, and, as a FIRST-CLASS HOTEL, affords unexceptionable accommodation for Private Families and Tourists, being in the immediate vicinity of the Railway, Post Office, Cathedral, Assembly Rooms, and the ruins of St. Mary's Abbey. AMERICAN TOURISTS are referred to the Hotel Register, Harper's Guide, &c. LIVERY AND POSTING ESTABLISHMENT. Under the patronage of H.R.H. the Prince of Wales. **J. PENROSE, Proprietor.**

HARKER'S YORK HOTEL,

ST. HELEN'S SQUARE,

YORK.

This long-established and first-class Family Hotel is in the best situation in the City, being nearest to the Minster, the Ruins of St. Mary's Abbey, &c., &c.; and within five minutes' walk of the Railway Station.

This Hotel is largely patronised by American Visitors.

P. MATTHEWS, Proprietor.

A page from "A Guide to Hotels of Europe", published in 1873.

ABOVE. The Ouse Bridge Inn on King's Staith in the 1890s.
BELOW. Blossom Street, just outside Micklegate Bar in the 1900s.

The Coach and Horses stood at the junction of Low Ousegate and Castlegate.

for their disposal? And without even waiting for his reply, gave him instructions to get rid of them. Maule had cause to rue the day he put into their minds the great advantage of the telephone, even to the extent of paying for the installation at the brewery himself. His private world of command and control had gone. Such were the unforeseen consequences of scientific progress.

24 May 1888

Taylor of Pocklington, who ran a daily bus and cab service between the White Swan in Goodramgate in York and Strensall camp, agreed to allow an advertisement for their beer to be printed on the back of his tickets so long as the firm paid for it. It was to mutual benefit, and an early example of the exploitation of a small and hitherto unperceived commercial entrepreneurial opportunity. Obviously Taylor thought so, and the partners recorded their view in the diary – 'cost £2 10s, cheap at the price and good value for money'.

* * *

The diary records a constant stream of public houses being offered to them on lease by their owners. These fell mainly into two categories – those belonging to landed estates whose proprietors were anxious to unload problems, and owner-occupiers wanting to exploit a successful house by leasing it for an assured rent. The difficulty with the first category, so far as the partners were concerned, was that the proprietors never spent any money on their properties, so they were in poor order and, given that the partners were averse to spending money even on the houses they owned, they recoiled at spending on houses they did not own. However, if they saw an opportunity to sell a good quantity of beer they averted their gaze from the dilapidation and hoped that something would turn up in the course of the lease to improve the situation. In the other category, the problem was to calculate accurately what quantity of beer they felt they could sell compared with what the owner sold or said he sold – not by any means the same figures, as the partners found out to their cost on several occasions.

Their deliberations, as recorded in the diary, over whether or not to take on a house from an owner-occupier always followed the same pattern. Monro would lead the opposition, declaring that it was well known that the trade was nothing like that asserted and that if it were, then it had been bought with low prices and after hours drinking – a statement confirmed by the others. Then there would be a period of silence on the matter, often followed by an entry that it had been agreed to take a lease because reports indicated that the firm's beer would be well received in the district and that they had no other outlet for their beer there. Then, after a year or so had passed, an entry would appear that, as he had said at the time (this could be from any one of the partners, regardless of his previously held view), the taking-on of this house was a 'disaster', the roof was falling in, the tenant was a drunkard who had not paid them for the last two or three deliveries and, what was more, the beer was undrinkable. Several immediate and choleric ripostes would follow, but nothing about the eventual outcome. One might be forgiven for thinking that a diary was being maintained on the domestic lives of a married couple.

The brewers' rush to secure tied outlets by purchase or lease had not gained ground in the provinces (as it had in the metropolis) and there were innumerable independent public houses among which the brewers could compete for trade. Also, the longer this prevailed, the better it suited the brewers' capital position, for they did not need to raise large sums to buy freeholds. None of the big local brewers, such as Tetley in Leeds or John Smith in Tadcaster, saw any need to increase their tied estates – in fact Tetley did not make any serious move towards acquiring a tied estate until after the First World War.

The urge for acquisition turned into hysteria in the 1950s, not out of rational consideration of the market or the licensing laws, but from the mistaken belief that considerable economies could be made by building huge breweries and closing small ones, by acquiring all the public houses in an area and then closing several and thereby forcing customers to go to those that remained, and by offering them only one type of beer in surroundings and at a price dictated by the brewery.

Not surprisingly, the same period saw a massive increase in the popularity of workingmen's clubs, where the beer was cheap and the atmosphere was closer to what the customer wanted. The boards of directors of large breweries had become obsessed with size to the detriment of any other consideration; in time it became apparent that the only economies had been in the short term, for they were quickly wiped out by huge increases in the overhead costs of transport and administration, not to mention by the loss of customers to the clubs.

The same companies that had trumpeted on about economies of scale were now leading the campaign to raise the retail price of beer. For the past 40 years the brewing industry has harboured a myth that small breweries are uneconomic. But this is not so. I myself ran a small publicly quoted brewery for over 20 years (from 1960 to 1986) and consistently brewed and sold beer more cheaply (and with the same margin) as the big breweries. However, the brewery ultimately suffered the fate of all such small companies – a larger brewery made a bid for the shares the holders could not refuse and, despite assurances to the contrary, it was closed within months and demolished. Beer prices were quickly hoisted to pay for the acquisition and the customers had no option but to accept the brewery's decision.

4 June 1888

The local newspapers had caught up with the march of progress at the brewery, though readers may have suspected that the articles were placed by a telephone company anxious to spread the word about its product and its usefulness to commerce. There was a lengthy report in the *York Herald* about the installation of a telephone link between the York office and Tadcaster brewery and how convenient it was to business; and an even longer report in the *Yorkshire Gazette* covered the same topic. Both reporters wrote of the pleasure of speaking through the telephone and marvelled at the 'clearness and distinctiveness with which the various questions put were instantly answered in a clear voice from the brewery at Tadcaster some nine miles distant'. The telephone line was actually 13 miles long, for some landowners had unfortunately failed to see the merits of the system in the same light as the telephone company did and refused access across their land. Nonetheless, one is left with the impression that the partners were at the vanguard of innovation in York and could see the virtues of the device – which perhaps an older generation could not. One wonders how these early telephone users began their conversations. Bell made his first telephone call using the nautical salutation of 'Ahoy', and it was only when the first telephone exchange was established in Connecticut that it was felt necessary to devise an accepted word to initiate a conversation. So 'Hello' was decreed, from the hunting call of 'Halloo' with acknowledgement to the phrase 'Here I am'. It is uncertain whether this piece of verbal etymology had crossed the Atlantic by the 1880s.

5 June 1888

The delights of the telephone were overshadowed by the partners' rage at discovering that no less than 18 railway wagons of beer were awaiting unloading at York railway station. Extra horses had to be hired to get the loads away and the men had to work all day Sunday.

They also considered the matter of Cartwright's brewery at Lincoln; they did not want the brewery itself and were only prepared to lease the houses. They gratuitously advised Cartwright to dispose of his brewery elsewhere.

7 June 1888

A cutting pasted into the diary from the *Standard* discussed the teetotal faction's demonstrations in Hyde Park against the licensing clauses in Gladstone's Local Government Reform Bill before the House of Commons. They were incensed, as only single issue reformers can be, that a liquor licence holder should be offered compensation if his licence were refused. The partners felt the teetotallers were going too far and were overreaching themselves in requiring abolition without financial redress of a right granted by law; they were sure there would be a reaction to this stand.

The demonstration was really concerned with the extension of the principle of local option throughout the country – that is, the granting of liquor licences on conditions determined locally, from complete bans to restricted licensing hours.

14 June 1888

At the York office the partners seemed to have constant problems with their grooms and their entries in the diary were regularly accompanied by moans and outbursts of indignation about them. Perhaps, as country gentlemen well versed in equine affairs, they felt that they were particularly well qualified to pass judgement on all matters pertaining to horses. A note was written that Shaw should be spoken to because he appeared 'to be getting more idiotic every day'. Apparently, according to an entry in another hand, Shaw had taken the bay mare to Strensall when she was very lame and, on being asked why he did this, had replied that she would never get any better. Brave words were expressed in the diary and one of the partners said that he would speak his mind despite upsetting Shaw. This was a rather remarkable statement given that the partners had never before shown any inhibition about stating their minds to anyone, whether employees or fellow colleagues.

A week later there was a note to the effect that the bay mare would have to be sold.

16 June 1888

They had received an intimation that old Mr Hotham had left York for a stay in Torquay. The entry had an aura of relief about it, as if they found comfort in both his absence and the distance. He had a habit of calling upon them in the office unannounced to collect his rent.

On the same day the modern wonder of the telephone suffered a natural catastrophe. The bell at the brewery was struck by lightning and shattered. When a thunderbolt struck the Minster in York 100 years later causing serious damage, the insurance company called it an 'act of God' and some people even gave credence to the idea that it might be divine displeasure at the appointment to the See of Durham. However, there was nothing written in the diary to suggest that the partners harboured any such views on the subject.

3 July 1888

It was a very wet day and there had been a terrible gale all night, so a review of the militia proposed at Strensall had to be cancelled. The partners had decorated the brewery drays and dressed up the horses for the occasion; but the effort was not wasted, for the draymen were sent round the city in a procession which was 'much admired by the population'.

4 July 1888

The defection of the American colonies was too recent for the day to be taken into the lore of the island race. Instead, the partners thought about their employees and not in favourable terms. They began by declaring Hale, the working brewer, to be an idiot; in this case it was enough to mark him such without reason. Allison, the foreman at York was disobeying 'all' orders and was constantly drunk. They gave orders for the old mare to be sent off to the kennels for slaughter and decided to advertise for two good draymen — first-class men with wages offered to secure men of this calibre. According to the job specification they were to be strangers, though quite how they were to be assessed as such was not set down.

5 July 1888

Some of them went to Newcastle-upon-Tyne to arrange the take-over of a lease of the Duke of Sutherland on the corner of High Friar Street and Clayton Street in the city centre and to pay over the valuation money to the outgoing tenant. Crombie, the firm's solicitor, had prepared an agreement for Burke and his wife to sign, which was done. They noted that it was a very wet day, that they got soaked through and that the house was very dirty.

On taking over the lease of the Duke of Sutherland public house, the partners had gone into their reasons and their underlying strategy for deciding to take this property. They needed a witness outlet to the acceptability of their beer in the city; they also needed a base for their traveller in the city, and a home for him, which all came together in this property. Burke, the employee (or more accurately his wife) was to be installed as manager and the other benefits would flow naturally. They carefully prepared an annual profit and loss account and, like many brewers in this situation, were convinced that their beer sales would be greater than what they were told they were at actual current sales of five hogsheads a week.

'*Debit*	
Piano and man to play	£52 1s 0d
Rent	£110 0s 0d
Interest on the valuation of £140	£7 0s 0d
Burke's wife at 10s a week	£26 0s 0d
Girl at 5s a week	£13 0s 0d
Gas, rates and taxes	£30 0s 0d
Beer and wine licence	£4 1s 0d
Strong lad to help bar	£26 0s 0d
Cost of ale (40 per cent)	£324 0s 0d
Tadcaster expenses (5 per cent)	£40 0s 0d
Carriage (say)	£60 0s 0d
Sundry expenses (say)	£20 0s 0d
	£712 2s 0d

Credit	
Sales per annum	£1075 0s 0d
Profit on wine, aerated waters and cigars	£25 0s 0d
	£1100 0s 0d
Balance profit	£388 2s 0d

N.B. The sales are taken at 6 barrels = 4 hogsheads per week, and this equals 216 gallons per week which at 6d per quart = 2s per gallon. As it is all KKK and IPA. The weekly takings should be therefore about £21 to £22.'

On the same day one of the old brewery mares was shot and died at once; Snary, the groom, reported the new one was sound and cheap at £30.

Troubles did not come singly on that day — it was noticed that Allanson had looked 'muddled' after the procession through York and was given his notice when he was sober, along with Brooks, both for drunkenness, and a resolution was made to replace them with good men. The wet weather did the firm some good, for Brett, their big rival from Manchester in supplying the military camps, did not show up at Strensall and left the field to them.

The underbrewer (Hale) was designated an idiot because, knowing the grinding rollers for the malt were faulty, he did not report the matter. Maule, the brewer, promised to attend to this and the partners agonized over the loss of profit.

An undated entry then followed, which simply read 'horse feeding'. It was menacing in its brevity and pregnant with passion on a matter all the partners, without exception, would claim as their own area of expertise. Sadly, the diary never took it up again.

Appalling weather continued throughout the summer of 1888; a note was inserted that Strensall camp was 'one large swamp'.

10 July 1888

The partners discussed the state of trade in Grimsby, where they had not long been operating; by and large they were satisfied, but the free-trade traveller was considered useless and dismissed. They also considered extending their business down the Lincolnshire coast and across the Wash to King's Lynn, transporting the beer by water from Gainsborough; in the end they dropped the thought as the person approaching them (Palmer) could not offer enough trade to cover the transport costs.

17 July 1888

They had looked at their hop stocks and their needs for the coming year. They had also taken note of the gossip about the hop harvest prospects, and quoted to themselves the adage 'When hops are one shilling a pound, lay in two years' stock.' Currently, they were ranging between 6d and 9d a pound and they decided to stock up with a year's supply. Maule the brewer was called over from Tadcaster and he suggested buying one-third foreign and two-thirds English hops, which would make good yearlings. Tripp, the general manager, was dispatched to London to do this, subject, as ever in the partners' instructions, to anything he might hear to change his mind. He caught the train down to London and stayed at the Great Northern Hotel, King's Cross, and returned the next day. He reported that as prices were rising, he had bought on the spot; he had secured 'some grand Burgundy hops' at 45s a hundredweight, which Maule had seen and approved. Following the review at Strensall, Colonel Braddell explained to Tripp that he would be giving up control of the canteens to Colonel Main, with whom he would put in a good word for the firm's beer.

18 July 1888

One of the partners noted that on passing through Huntington he had found three of the brewery drays outside a public house and the draymen inside enjoying themselves. Discretion made him pass on, but he hurried back to the office and told one of the clerks to find out who the men were, and then to tell them that any draymen stopping at Huntington pubs would face immediate dismissal.

A visit to Tadcaster satisfied them that the new well sunk for them by Isler was progressing satisfactorily; he was going to charge them £150 for the job. Then one of them looked up the diary for 1882 and found that Smalley sank the other well there for £33. There followed mutual recrimination.

They returned to the subject of making donations to feasts at various of their houses; they considered they were increasing alarmingly – not surprising really, as free beer had a habit of creating this effect, but their capacity for simple wonder at nature never diminished. They noted, on enquiry, that some tenants still had feasts and free beer, whereas others did not. They realized, in writing, that a feast was the method of thanking customers for their patronage through the tenant. They also came to the conclusion that feasts were too ingrained in the customs of the licensed trade to be stopped.

23 July 1888

The partners had decided to take the tenancy of the Queen's Hotel, Saltburn by the Sea, at a rent of £150 yearly. Trade there ran at about £700 in beer and £300 in wines and spirits. It was noted that it was a large hotel and that only one half was open. They eventually took it at £175 rent.

The partners had purchased the Stamford Bridge brewery of the late Mr W. Mason and, on visiting the tenants of the public houses, found a complete refusal by them to sign any new tenancy agreements on the basis that they had been in their houses for decades and had never been asked to sign agreements. The partners accepted the situation.

25 July 1888

The weather continued to be 'terribly wet and the hay harvest was spoilt'; what was really alarming was a report that the volunteers would not come up for their camp on 4 August if the weather went on like this. Bad news indeed.

They thought about the annual 'do' for the employees. Instead of a dinner, as heretofore, there would be a trip to Scarborough; all agreed it was a good idea. The annual feast for employees traditionally consisted of a gargantuan meal and a copious supply of beer and, like the suppers for farmers and landed estate workers, took place between getting the hay in and harvest time, when working the land was at its lowest level and the weather was fine and warm. Only employees attended; no wives, no lady friends, no spirits, no wine – just beef and beer and pudding. It was the best meal of the year for most of those attending and they looked forward to it with intense pleasure; a malting floor was usually cleaned out for the purpose, for it was the biggest readily available area outside the brewery buildings. One of the tenants, well known for his catering abilities, arranged things; the brewer brewed up some especially strong beer, for that was what was expected, and of course the men talked about it afterwards – it was an advertising opportunity not to be missed. For them to say that they were paralytically drunk after so many pints filled their hearers with envy and a desire to taste the beer for themselves. As for the food, it was scarce enough at home, particularly meat, and to say that they had filled themselves with slice after slice was also a cause for pride. They were carted home in the small hours on the brewery drays, the drivers as drunk as their passengers, but the horses knew the way.

* * *

This annual event changed with the coming of the railways, for now people could travel great distances and come back again within a day; also it was an attraction for men who had never before been out of their village or out of York to go to far-off places, especially to the seaside. Indeed, unless they had been soldiers or sailors, they would have had no opportunity to do so. It all really began with the Great Exhibition of 1851, at which the masses first heard about the activities of Mr Thomas Cook and became inspired by the idea of travel. Again, following the example of Bass at Burton-on-Trent, the partners were among the first to replace the static feast with an employees' outing, which usually consisted of a highly organized trip to Blackpool on several hired trains.

This went on until the early 1950s, when the social upheavals following the war made all-male affairs and drunkenness unacceptable. For a while female employees, whose numbers on the breweries' staff lists had increased considerably, were permitted to come on the trips. But this quickly caused friction among the wives of male employees, who suspected the worst, and often with justification. Also, the drunkenness, vomiting and unruly behaviour became quite intolerable to the police, railway officials, coach drivers, restaurateurs and hotel staff, who began to refuse to take bookings.

The growth in continental holidays changed the attitudes of the ordinary lower classes towards enjoyment and this, combined with the hostility of wives and girlfriends, brought an end to the trips, which were replaced by dinner dances held either in hotels, public dance halls with suitable facilities or (much more exciting) in converted maltings. The wheels of change had gone full circle, though this time round the brewery spent more money on the dances and standards were much higher. The maltings were transformed for the evening into fairyland palaces, and the ladies appreciated the effort. At first all drinks of all kinds were freely available with the usual results and a lot of late night unpleasantness, plus trouble with drunken driving of motorcars, now increasingly being issued to employees by the brewery. So, apart from free wine at dinner, all other drink had to be paid for at discounted prices and, to cut down on drunken driving, hired motor coaches would pick up the guests at fixed points and deliver them back to their homes at the end of the evening. Of course, there was still trouble, but it was contained.

Then, with the growth of the enormous brewery companies, the feeling of being together in one society vanished, with such loyalty as survived being given only to one's immediate workmates, and the attraction of the annual dinner dance or communal get-together, faded. Today, except in the small brewery companies, this entertainment and diffused thank-you to the employees has gone and will not return. As I write, the severe economic situation has put paid to big company-expense entertainment, including for senior staff, though many smaller companies still recognize the economic advantage of such occasions and continue to hold the kinds of feast the partners tried so hard to abandon. But for most people now a night in front of the television is preferable to a dance and dressing-up for an occasion is considered old fashioned. Dances have become convulsive gyrations to loud music in solitude and darkness, with conversation and observation of the passing scene impossible. In fact, what attraction is there for any person, other than the young and single, to have a night out?

* * *

30 July 1888

They noted that Mrs Blakey had died.

Amidst all their concentration on supplying the Strensall camps and keeping the officers and mess sergeants happy, Thompson, tenant of the Waggon & Horses, Gillygate, York, came in to the office and said he could not make a living. His profit was around £269 a year and he wanted to be free of his tie. They were amazed and gave him short shrift. The telephone ceased working as well.

4 August 1888

Mr Hotham called in; he wanted his rents and the interest on the balance of his loan to the firm. He said he wanted 6 per cent interest rate if the loan was to stay. They were taken aback.

6 August 1888

The partners were pleased with the malt yield of the Dalmatian barley at Dale's malthouse — 423 pounds per bushel.

They noted in the diary that while they were pleased with the Strensall camp trade, the tied houses in York were doing very poorly, with tenants calling to complain about the competitors selling beer more cheaply. The complaint seemed to be confined to York itself, and centred on the brewers Smith, Brett & Hunt selling at enormous discounts or sanctioning the long pull (i.e. giving beer away in the outlets).

The sinking of the new well at the brewery was proceeding satisfactorily, except that a chisel was lost in the borehole and would have to be recovered.

7 August 1888

Telephone communication was restored and advice given that it should be spoken into an inch or so away; the instrument was changed for a new model.

8 August 1888

Thompson called in again and said he would stay on as tenant of the Waggon & Horses! On the same day old Mr Hotham came in for his money and was asked to sign a receipt in the diary; he was also offered a capital sum off his mortgage but declined.

9 August 1888

The firm's outing to Scarborough was arranged for Thursday 16 August. Tripp, the general manager, negotiated terms with Mrs Nevile of the Imperial Hotel, to provide dinner, with three pints of beer each, at 3s 6d per person. He also arranged cheap tickets with the North Eastern Railway Company and had given notice in the papers that the offices would be closed. Some 76 employees would leave York at 10.02 a.m. and return at 8.00 p.m. from Scarborough.

10 August 1888

Tripp appeared before the magistrates at Guildhall to speak on behalf of Dale, the tenant of the Nag's Head, Fossgate, accused of harbouring prostitutes. The magistrates were persuaded it was carelessness on Dale's part and the case against him was dismissed.

11 August 1888

It was reported that the Tadcaster well was now down to 44 feet, with 10 feet of water in it; the chisel had been found but not yet recovered.

13 August 1888

Tripp saw Colonel Braddell at Strensall to arrange a changeover, and the general came up and said that he had been deeply impressed with all that the firm had done and that there had not been one single complaint. He added that he hoped the camp had been of some benefit to the firm. So the 1888 season of military camps had been worth the attention given to them by the firm. Tripp was invited to have a cigar with Colonel Main in his mess.

A scale was devised for rewarding agents and travellers for introducing tied houses to the firm: (1) For leasehold properties of three years, 5 per cent on trade for the previous three years up to £500, with 2.5 per cent above that figure. (2) For houses with yearly tenancies, the commission would be 2.5 per cent up to £500 and 1.25 per cent above that. The observation was made that unless an incentive was offered, travellers would not devote time to getting tied house trade. Brum & Son sent samples of their new Moravian barley; considered very poor; price 38s and 39s.

14 August 1888

There was a familiar complaint of sour ale from a tenant; investigation showed it to be gyle 140, and the brewery had reached gyle 250. A lecture on rotation of stock was given. Also, customers had changed their tastes and wanted new ale not old, as used to be the fashion.

15 August 1888

Several people were interested in taking the Queen's Hotel, Saltburn by the Sea, but £500 was needed for the ingoing. Eventually it was let to W. Smith at £120 rent and three months' notice either side. He was pronounced an excellent man. Tripp announced he was going to Scotland for his fortnight's holiday. The partners wrote up the diary themselves and approved Tripp's suggestions *en bloc*.

22 August 1888

Monro and Parker 'had it out' with Hotham about his mortgage, and he gave in and agreed to abide by the existing deed; he was again offered £700 off the balance and refused it.

8 September 1888

It was reported that the new well was now 66 feet down and into blue clay and that the men were getting through six feet a day. Also, the new grinding rollers were working well.

12 September 1888

Mr Hotham called into the office and said he would like the interest on his mortgage shortly and £1000, not the £700 offered, of capital. He was told that he could have this money at any time after the end of the month, to which he agreed.

13 September 1888

The partners considered their hop stocks and their desire to have a year's supply in hand. They found that prices had risen and quality had gone down; finally they bought 26 pockets of Kenward 1886 Sussex at 46s and 17 bales of Bohemians 1887 at 70s, and resolved that that would have to do for the present.

17 September 1888

Tripp noted that Allanson, a friend living in Exeter, had married Miss Rowlett, the daughter of a canon of Exeter cathedral, and a cousin of Colonel Allardice, the commanding officer at the Beverley depot. She had been persuaded to write to him about giving the firm a supply to the Beverley barracks.

18 September 1888

Isler & Company, contractors for the new well, were sent £100 on account, and trial pumping over the weekend showed no diminution of supply in either the old or new borehole. The well was taken over from the contractors on the 20th. Analysis showed the two wells to be the same, with the new one having slightly harder water. The old well was 54 feet deep and the new one 70 feet.

It was noted that Tom Newton, paid out on 3 September, was seen riding about York, booted and spurred and with white breeches on a great black 15-stone hunter. Parker had heard he had gone into the wine trade.

20 September 1888

There were disturbing reports from the brewery of beer returns amounting to some 700 barrels by the end of the month, compared with 900 at the same time last year. The partners felt the loss would be immense. One entire gyle had gone wrong and was coming back from every outlet to which it had been sent. The brewers were instructed to look into the question of preservatives, and they noted that the one they used, Gileman's P, helped the position very little.

It was a dismal time all round with plenty of houses to let and fewer applicants than ever before. A great number of houses continued to be on offer to the firm from all over the North. They were mainly leasehold and the tenants, having worked up a trade, were anxious to sell their leases to a brewery and move on to the next house to do a repeat performance. For example, the Nag's Head, fully licensed, situated at the bottom of George's Stairs, Quayside, Newcastle-upon-Tyne, leased by Barras from December 1887 and on offer by him because he was taking over his father's house in the city centre, had the following beer purchases:

Bass & Company	
December 1887	£30
January 1888	£16
February	£46
March	£51
April	£71
May	£53
June	£50
July	£49

From other brewers	£85
August to November (estimate)	£200
plus wines and spirits	£100

Barras stated his takings were between £22 and £25 weekly.

The owner was Mr A. Reid, a printer, who wanted £80 yearly rent for a three-year lease. The firm agreed to an annual tenancy and thereafter three months' notice on either side and an ingoing valuation of £100. A manager was appointed, John Winter, formerly valet to Mr Wylam for five years and at one time with Parker (when he was with a Newcastle-upon-Tyne bank).

1 October 1888

The firm's year ended the previous day. The books were closed and stocks taken, including the agencies – 'We will now prepare for the auditors.'

2 October 1888

A new chief constable had been appointed for York city; he was said to be a teetotaller and was from Shrewsbury.

3 October 1888

The staff were preparing for the auditors. They had been through the ledgers and found bad debts of £460 (in 1887 they had been £542). They were pleased with this, but added the caution that the firm could hardly expect such a low amount to continue. They also pointed out that they had included a loss of £40 on the canteen at Strensall camp in that it cost the firm £240 and the engineers only paid £200, so the balance had to be written off.

Perhaps gleefully (and nervously) they noted that J. Smith of Tadcaster, the brewer, had lost £600 from a traveller in Wakefield. It was also noted that Tom Newton had joined a firm of wine and spirit merchants and had been to Hagley to ask him for some orders.

4 October 1888

Tripp went to the Teeside area on a day visit; he took in Saltburn and Stockton districts, looking at prospective outlets. He left Stockton at 11.00 p.m. and got into York at 2.00 a.m.

9 October 1888

Audit reported to be going well.

10 October 1888

Mrs Nicholson, who had recently taken over the Turk's Head, York, showed Monro her spirits. The whisky jar had been filled up with paraffin oil after the valuation had been taken. Surely, asked Monro, the firm are not going to stand for this sort of thing? He went on to suggest that the outgoing tenant be made to pay for the whole of the spirits and even sued in court for it, and that Charlesworth's brother be held down by a couple of draymen and be made to drink a pint of paraffin. A reply was soon written into the diary; Tripp said that the valuers had tested the spirits and they were good. Any paraffin must have been added afterwards, by which time Mrs Nicholson was responsible. A hard case, but the brewery was powerless. The whole stock of beer and spirits was only £4 1s 6d! So the loss was very little.

It was noted that Mr Beckett had written in concerning his account. He had asked for a detailed statement and wanted to know who ordered the supplies and to where they were sent. It was further noted that he always made a fuss. He must have been the Beckett of Beckett's Bank of York, with an eye for detail.

12 October 1888

The audit was still proceeding: 'We were all here again last evening, until close upon 12.00 p.m., and will have all ready for Akers when he comes on Tuesday at 9.00 a.m.' It had been the heaviest preparatory audit ever; sales being 22.5 per cent up on last year. However, every book would be written up and off and Akers should easily be finished by Friday or Saturday next – it was hoped.

Points of interest on the year's sales:

To 30 September 1888, 27,544 barrels sold for £55,533
To 30 September 1887, 22,595 barrels sold for £44,765

According to the diary figures, there had been an increase of 22.5 per cent in ale sales; although the mathematics are perhaps approximate, the trend was in the right direction. Returns of unsaleable ale, too, were better – 716 barrels in 1888 to 782 in 1887. The opening of the firm's Grimsby depot had proceeded well. They had worked on the basis of selling 37 barrels a week, and achieved 57 in the nine months of operation. Overall, their total sales of all intoxicating liquors had been £72,847, against the previous year of £58,435, an increase of 25 per cent.

The all-important trade with the military camps at Strensall amounted to:

Canteens for the troops, less returns	£9514
Messes for officers and NCOs	£2854

Economies were being effected in the feeding of the horses; a chopper had been bought and hay and good oat straw were being mixed and chopped in equal amounts.

Then there was an intriguing entry in pencil – 'Tom Newton's time was up at Bilbro' on 11th instant. Mrs T intends "reproducing" in three weeks, consequently Hornsey the agent deals leniently with them.'

18 October 1888

They purchased 2000 quarters of Wallachian barley at 28s 6d FOB Hull, and considered the sample very nice.

20 October 1888

Akers finished the audit the previous night and was able to have a quiet morning to explain details to the firm. Tied trade showed a serious falling off and the replacement with free trade would mean much extra expense.

Meanwhile Maule, the brewer, went off to the London Brewers' Exhibition and discussed with Faulkner, a consultant brewing chemist, the use and extra use of Indian flaked malt. This must have been part of a cost-saving drive, for at a meeting at the brewery dire warnings were delivered about savings and attention drawn to the scandalous and careless way of handling thermometers – they had cost £50 in the previous year. Wages were examined and a list put into the diary:

Brewing men	
Marsden, tun room and night (weekly)	£1 3s 0d
Pratt, ditto	£1 3s 0d
Smith, R. ditto	£1 1s 0d
Carrol, E. ditto	£1 1s 0d
Walker, copper	£1 3s 0d
Marsden, H., grinder	19s 0d
Machan, grains	19s 0d
Milk, racking	19s 0d
Fowler, ditto	19s 0d
Smith, J., ditto	18s 0d
Smith, H., yeast presser	10s 0d
Lazenby, barrel washer	18s 0d
Hodgson, ditto	18s 0d
Cracken, ditto	18s 0d
Smith, A., boy	8s 0d
Hale, T., copper/underbrewer	£1 10s 0d
Drayman	
Shilletor, J.	£1 0s 0d
Coopers	
Vine Street Union trade man	£2 5s 0d
Lyman, on piece work	£2 2s 0d
Clerks	
Groves, H., general foreman	£2 0s 0d
Elliott, A., office clerk	£1 5s 0d
Boiler man	
Wilson	£1 5s 0d
Total	£40 11s 0d

The wage bill exceeded the previous year by £1 15s 5d, so Cracken had to go. And it was felt that there were too many in the tun room and on at night, so one of them would have to come and assist in loading the railway trucks when busy there.

27 October 1888

Tripp went on his travels to ensure the trade of the military for 1889. He caught the train to Leicester after leaving the Brewers' Exhibition in London, and visited the Glen Parva barracks, where he saw the canteen steward and Sergeant Major Vesey, Colonel Utterson and Major Moir being away. Vesey confirmed the arrangement for two barrels of beer to be sent as a trial, and he was sure the men would like it. Tripp gathered that the account was worth £70 a month at a time when the regiment's strength was low, and it should rise to £100. He was concerned at the cost of rail freight charges to Leicester at 21s 8d per ton, and he had seen the agent in York with a view to a special price; freight loomed large in the costing of beer cartage, and it was a constant struggle at Tadcaster to require the brewer to keep his brewings in line with demand, so that old beer did not have to be carried back from depots to the brewery. Discounts by the railway companies had to be pressed for by customers, and this work was constantly engaged in by Tripp, the firm being a regular user; he did in fact achieve a reduced rate from the Midland Railway agent for the haulage from Tadcaster to Leicester.

He then left for Derby at 3.00 p.m. and got a cab to the barracks, where he saw Quartermaster Lynch, whom he counted as a friend of the firm's and who held the key to the situation because he would be assuming the canteen presidency in December and undoubtedly would do his best to secure the beer supply for them. He had tea with Lynch and then called upon Sergeant Major Croker, who promised his mess supply at Strensall in 1889 if the regiment went to Strensall, and even if it went to Buxton, the position would be the same. Tripp got to York at 9.38 p.m.

30 October 1888

The partners were pleased to note that the 'Income Tax People' had accepted the statement of income at £5275 as correct and with tax at 6d in the £, tax due in January would be £131 17s 6d.

1 November 1888

The cost-cutting exercises continued. The practice of offering a glass of spirits or port to visitors to the offices was considered very expensive and a switch to beer served from a cask was implemented. It was reported that seven out of ten visitors preferred a glass of beer.

Even the costs of shives and pegs for the beer barrels were looked at. Deighton & Company of York, the traditional suppliers, at 1s 3d per gross, would not budge their price, and Bramley of New Wortley in Leeds was quoting one shilling carriage paid. A warning was delivered to them.

It was decided that there would be no rises in the clerks' salaries. They would have to make do with overtime.

The brewery travellers' and agents' costs came under scrutiny. Scott, who looked after Wakefield, was asked to reduce his expenses. He suggested fetching the beer supplies from the station if he could have a horse and float with which to do it and to deliver to customers. Shepherd, another traveller, had to give up his horse and trap and was told to walk and use the train, as he would get no more salary or expenses. The estimated saving would be £60 per annum. He was given a target to increase his trade from 16 to 20 barrels a week.

2 November 1888

It was noted that Stott, 'the teetotaller', on the Watch Committee, which was made up of those justices who dealt with liquor licensing matters, had been ousted from the Walmgate ward in the city elections in favour of Wrightson, an Independent. Stott was considered a very narrow-minded man.

An interesting note stated that 'there are several sleepers, or dead corns, in this season's Yorkshire barleys; more than for several years past. This fact will prevent the use of hard grain, whether rice or maize, when we come to use the malt.' This obviously explained the rice and maize purchases.

6 November 1888

Burke, the Tyneside traveller, brought Smithfield from Jarrow to the office; Smithfield had a free house and bought eight hogsheads of beer from the firm every fortnight. He wanted to sell the house and was asking £13,000 for an annual trade of £6500. The partners reckoned it was the best house ever brought to their notice for purchase. They tried hard to get him to rent it to them but he was adamant about wanting to sell. They noted that the trade required six men to handle it and that the volume was 20 hogsheads a week of KKK and BBA.

8 November 1888

The partners remarked that they had no brewery pupils in view and that those then in the brewery would soon end their stay. They put an advertisement in the *Field* and the *Yorkshire Post* anonymously and had one reply.

9 November 1888

Hudson, the tenant of the Blacksmith's Arms in Dunnington, owed £30 on rent and would not pay, so the firm put in the bailiff. He then agreed to pay £15 in a month, plus the bailiff's charges; the firm agreed to let him stay.

The same situation applied to Amos, the tenant of the White Swan in Skeldergate, York. However, there was no offer to settle and the bailiff proposed to take all he could and to evict him. Harman, the tenant of the Cricketer's Arms, Tanner Row, York, had left the house to avoid his creditors; the bailiff was put in to protect the brewery.

The City Council met on the previous day and Alderman Agar was made lord mayor. One of the firm's tenants, P. Matthews, was made sheriff. It was noted that the Watch Committee would be much altered in the trade's favour, for with Wrightson elected for Walmgate ward, the teetotaller Stott was now out of the way and Lindberg appointed to the committee in his place – 'Lindberg being a gentleman, and one who takes a glass like the rest'. Agar being now lord mayor, his place was taken on the committee by Alderman Close – 'a man whom we can all trust to see that justice is done'.

10 November 1888

Maule, the brewer, pointed out that he would need two new squares for brewing to meet next summer's trade expectation; also, to use raw grain with success he had to have a second underback to dissolve any traces of starch, for the iodine solution showed the presence of crude starch with rice or maize. They agreed to write to Briggs & Company for a quotation.

The new well, with so much pumping, was producing cloudy water. On being informed, Isler replied that this would be so, but with rest it would be all right.

G. H. Siddons, the double bass player at the theatre, applied for the tenancy of the Shoulder of Mutton.

12 November 1888

To combat the buying-out by tied-trade tenants, Park, the traveller looking after the military canteens, was given the extra duty of calling on tied tenants suspected of breaking the tie.

The firm had undertaken the management of the Strensall military canteen and in the first month it made a net profit of £7 10s 1d on the grocery side and £15 10s 0d on beer and stout. The firm was very pleased with its trade at the Queen's Hotel, Saltburn by the Sea. The 2000 quarters of foreign barley purchased had arrived at Hull, and it was arranged for Wood to bring it to York by water at 10d per quarter.

14 November 1888

Tripp went to Jarrow to see Smithfield and went over his house, and was much impressed. He noted that the cellar held 100 hogsheads. However, he would not lease, only sell.

20 November 1888

The partners considered the attitude of the new chief constable and came to the conclusion that he was a very sharp man against licensed victuallers, and a lot of trouble could be anticipated. The previous night at the council meeting, the radical teetotal section moved a similar resolution to that recently issued in London, namely that whenever a man is taken up drunk the police were to try to find out where he had got his drink and then to proceed against the publican from whom it was obtained. The firm thought it ought to issue a warning to its tenants that if they were convicted of supplying drunks the firm would be very severe; they sent out a circular, warning against breaches of any part of the licensing laws. 'Only yesterday' the partners wrote in the diary, 'Burley who had held a licence for 20 years, applied for a protection order and the chief constable opposed it because he considered Burley's wife was not a fit person to leave in the house.'

21 November 1888

Old Mr Hotham called into the office and took up his mortgage interest, plus £700 off the capital.

22 November 1888

They got private information that the police intended a raid on betting houses in York; word was sent out to tenants suspected of betting.

* * *

There were frequent references in the diary to how savings could be made in the operation of the business and calculations were set out to uphold the suggestions being put forward. These items were mostly initiated by Tripp, the general manager. When the partners ran the business directly, they were inclined to air opinions, not to say prejudices, that were intuitive and unsubstantiated. Tripp's arrival introduced substance and orderliness to the proposals and undoubtedly led to more rational decision making. Furthermore, he followed up decisions and actions to see if they were working as expected. His presence and appointment were timely.

27 November 1888

It was reported that Park, deputed to uncover erring tenants, had at last caught one who offered him a glass of port wine when he had bought none from the brewery for months. This was the only case Park had managed to uncover since his appointment. Either the tenants were too wily for him or purchasing outside the tie was less prevalent than they suspected; or perhaps Park was not a very good sleuth.

28 November 1888

Lord Zetland, the brother of C. T. Dundas, a partner, was

agreeable to letting the houses on his estate to the firm as they became vacant. He stated that all negotiations were to be made through the Zetland estate office at Saltburn by the Sea (whose agent was Mr W. J. Moscrop), or through Mr C. Newcomen, of Olliver, Richmond.

1 December 1888

An estimate was received from Briggs that the underback would cost £20, overflow to backs £10, and two dropping squares £130. The estimate was accepted subject to the firm getting six months' credit.

There was another interesting and opaque note – that the partners had heard on good authority that Newton and Anderson had been in London seeing counsel preparatory to legal action, and that they were so sure of winning that Anderson was advancing money to Newton himself. Anderson was his solicitor.

7 December 1888

The partners learned that the North Eastern Railway Company was surveying for a branch line at Castleford and that its route might pass through its maltings and employee's house there. They considered they might do well out of this by requiring the company to purchase their property entirely, and for the firm to operate from Wakefield, which was a notion they had entertained for some time. Sadly, it did not come to pass because the railway company decided to abandon the scheme.

10 December 1888

The new chief constable was living up to his reputation, as the partners soon found out. Kitchin, the second drayman and tenant of the Crispin Arms, Church Lane, North Street, York, came into the office to state he had received a summons for keeping his house as a brothel. He said he was quite unaware of anything like this in his house and denied the accusation *in toto*. On investigation by Tripp, it turned out that his wife, with whom he had lived for 11 years, was not his wife (they had never been married in church) and the firm had never known this fact. It was immediately apparent to them that the summons would be that much harder to fight. They consulted their solicitor, Dale, and at the hearing applied for an adjournment, which was opposed by the chief constable and refused by the bench (Messrs Agar & Mattheson). Dale in turn refused to go on with the case and after much argument it was stood over until later in the week.

Riley-Smith called in at the office and was shown the new malt, which he pronounced the best and 'free-est' Yorkshire barley malt he had seen that season.

11 December 1888

Tripp was giving very serious thought to the implications of the Crispin Arms case, for if Kitchin as licensee was convicted, the licence would be lost under the provisions of section 15 of the Licensing Act of 1872. It was known that the chief constable in conjunction with the Teetotal Party meant to make an example of everyone and to 'get each licence knocked on the head'. Tripp looked around for help and approached Mr Tomlinson-Walker and James Melrose, members of the Watch Committee, and asked them to be present when the case was resumed.

Tripp recorded in the diary his fears that licensed-house owners were at the mercy of their tenants' behaviour in their houses because their activities could result in the loss of licences and the loss of value of the premises, despite all efforts to control them. For instance, they had no inkling of what Kitchin had appeared to be up to at the Crispin Arms.

The firm's surveyor, Tarran, was asked to prepare a plan of the house, so as to show plainly to the magistrates at the hearing the layout of the rooms.

12 December 1888

Tripp continued his lobbying on the Crispin Arms case. He approached every member of the Watch Committee personally to ask them to be on the bench 'so that fair hearing may be had', and most agreed to do so. Tripp enlisted the aid of the Country Brewers' Society and got its solicitors' advice (free of cost, he added). Dale, the solicitor, and he looked up relevant reported cases and also got some advice from Crombie, a well-known local lawyer (again free of cost). Amidst this legal turmoil, Tripp saw the National Telephone Company's manager from Leeds and agreed these charges:

York to Tadcaster (line rental)	£20 per annum
York to Strensall	£30 per annum
Connection to York exchange	£10 per annum

13 December 1888

Notice was served on the firm that the North Eastern Railway Company intended to obtain an Act of Parliament to acquire the Lord Raglan public house, the brewery offices, stores and employee's house in Castleford.

Monro came into his own again. He wrote the intended course of action in red ink – dissent from the proposition and instruct parliamentary counsel to insist that the railway company take the firm's entire property holding, which included waste land stretching to the canal. Furthermore, all the partners should be aware of the matter and give their written authority for Parker and Monro to deal with it.

Tripp was to ascertain what the neighbouring landowners thought about it. Pipe, the firm's local employee, thought the North Eastern Railway Company would not get anywhere because the Midland Railway Company, whose line also passed through Castleford, had a bill before Parliament putting forward a line to go the other way, and that bill was supported by the Castleford local board.

14 December 1888

They lost the Crispin Arms case after a five-hour hearing. The licence was revoked and Dale gave notice of appeal. He had attempted to get the licence transferred before the hearing, but the application had been refused on the grounds that it was transparently bogus. There was collective breast-beating in the office – the iniquity of the law, the power of the tenant of a public house to ruin the owner, the impeccable character of Kitchin, whose reference had been signed by well-known Clifton people, never a complaint about him and now this!

17 December 1888

Tripp met Dale and they agreed to send a report to the Country Brewers' Society's solicitors so that they could get Candy's (Queen's Counsel) opinion on the likely success of an appeal. It was noted that the case, if remitted to Quarter Sessions, would be heard at York before the recorder, Price.

Monro had been testing the water in London on the Castleford matter and had received advice that the railway company had to take all the firm's property – 'a company may not knock down a man's house and yet leave his garden'.

18 December 1888

'Paid beer duty this day four days overdue; new collector seems in a hurry'. 'It is the new collector who is so fussy re duty. He has only been here two months.'

19 December 1888

Candy advised there was only very slight hope of success on appeal; the case was therefore dropped. The black mare, always ill and lame, was sold to an Edinburgh man for £21. She cost £28 two years previously; the sale was considered a good get-out.

20 December 1888

Monro called in at York and wrote in the diary that the yard was worse than any ploughed field, with mud and muck everywhere – on casks, on the malting floors, in three offices – disgusting. He recommended that Parker's gravel be removed and cobbles be put down. He then left his Christmas address – Ketteringham Park, Wymondham, Norfolk – the home of the Boileau family.

Monro went to see the chief constable about the tenant of the Market Tavern, who in the view of the firm was not running his business well. He reported he was most civil and promised to help the firm. It was a good meeting, thought Monro, and he intended to invite him out to dinner because he was a very gentleman-like man 'and we must get on the right side of him'.

24 December 1888

They appended some notes on tied-trade sales in recent years:

To 30 September 1884[*]	£32,316
To 30 September 1885 (31,185)[**]	£34,480
To 30 September 1886 (28,815)	£32,170
To 30 September 1887 (29,600)	£32,542
To 30 September 1888 (26,378-31,055)[***]	£35,513

They noted the fall in the York trade over the years.

They listed all their houses doing £400 or more annually in sales, being 14 in number. They also listed their worst houses, ten in number, doing under £75 annually, which would have to go.

The best house for trade was the New Inn, Featherstone, at £994; the worst the Shoulder of Mutton, Shambles, York, at £28.

26 December 1888

'One or two telegrams today for beer; we gave them attention and closed the offices.'

28 December 1888

Lawson, manager of Carter & Company's brewery at Knottingley, was sent over to York to offer to buy the Lancs & Yorks house at Knottingley. This was because they had learnt that the new tenant was to be Saul and they were afraid that he would take all the trade from their own hotel opposite. He was told that they had no intention of selling but that if they named a price the firm would consider it. They decided, if Carter was interested, that they would ask for £2500, having given £700 for it in 1884.

* * *

At the end of 1888 the diaries lost their human interest. As a set of books they went on until 1903, but only to record formal decisions and adherence to the legal requirements of the Companies Acts that there should be a record that meetings had

[*] York and Newcastle trade.
[**] With Castleford, Rotherham and Wakefield trade.
[***] With Grimsby trade.

been held, resolutions passed, accounts presented and that the auditors were satisfied with the state of the books. Private thoughts were no longer revealed and neither were hopes, fears or disagreements with colleagues. Bold declarations of incautious beliefs, usually reserved for the privacy of a man's home and to his wife alone, the intemperate outbursts and the racy language all ceased. Images of long-dead men no longer came alive through their written words. Motions were put forward and passed without dissent. Meetings opened and meetings closed.

In 1887 the partners had appointed Howard Tripp, of Scarborough, as their general manager; the two partners in the limelight of the diary entries had assumed their roles in 1879, and in their own fashion, had put the firm on its feet, and built it a new brewery in Tadcaster. Undoubtedly they felt nine years of leadership had blunted their zest for the commercial fray and, anyway, horses and racing were of increasing interest to them. The third dominant partner, who had entered in 1875 and left in 1889, selling his York residence at Clifton to Parker, vanished from the records. They perhaps missed his abrasive attitude, for now they had nothing to provoke them into making entries in the diary. By 1890 the old acerbity, high indignation and impetuous judgement had gone, and the handwritten entries down to 1903 became more and more impersonal, until they finished completely. Milner devoted himself to his political career, married and went to live in Buckinghamshire. Parker tired of the York scene, understood he was likely to be nominated sheriff of the city, which neither his temperament nor his pocket relished, and departed for London in 1907. The firm had become a limited company in 1894, the shareholding diffused among many strangers, albeit to the financial benefit of the partners. It was controlled from London, and it was the end of an era.

4

Expansion, 1889–1890

1 January 1889

Tripp had heard that Sam Smith of Tadcaster was tired of his brewery, so he wrote to him for an appointment and arranged a meeting at Meanwood, Leeds, at which an offer for £35,000 was considered for his brewery, malthouses and 21 houses, plus stock, book debts and loose plant at a valuation of about £10,000. The sale price would remain outstanding for 21 years at 5 per cent interest. On reflection, it was felt that £25,000 was nearer the mark. His tied trade was over £6000, rents were £550 and discount to tied trade was 10 per cent. Book debts were £4000. If the firm was interested, Smith would come to York to talk about it. He was adamantly against any leasing proposition.

Monro, as ever a knowing fellow, reported that Smith banked with Beckett's Bank for both his Leeds and Tadcaster businesses.

4 January 1889

Monro had a further private talk with the chief constable, who advised against sacking two of the female tenants, for he had nothing against their houses and would give prior notice if he had reason to suspect any of the firm's tenants. He went on to say that 'there are many people in York who think public houses are the gates of Hell, but I am not of that opinion, and think working men should have respectable inns to go to.'

The town clerk had indicated that the firm should pay a toll on the pig market being run behind one of the York houses and had said that unless this was paid the market would have to shut.

Terms were agreed with Snarry, the veterinary, for examining the horses at £1 5s 0d per horse per year; hired horses *pro rata*. At an average of ten horses, the cost would be £12 10s 0d yearly, plus charges for examining new horses.

The partners were of the opinion that the Californian hops, if up to scratch and purchased at under £6 a quarter, would make the firm independent well into May 1890.

10 January 1889

Parker ordered 15 tons of whinstone chips for the brewery yard.

The telephone at Tadcaster had a bell which could not be heard, even though the exchange had been ringing for ten minutes. Either the bell should be shifted or a lad employed at one shilling a day to work close by and listen for it.

Parker, who was keeping the diary while Tripp was away, noted that while Ashton, the tenant of the Ham & Firkin, York, had been attending court, a drunk tramp had entered the house and fallen asleep in the bar. He was found by a constable and was hauled out and given seven days. Ashton understood that he was to be prosecuted for having a drunk on his premises. Parker told him to see Dale, the solicitor, about the matter and added the observation that 'the life of these men is becoming unbearable' — presumably referring to licensees under the regime of the new chief constable.

12 January 1889

Monro recorded that he had ordered eight octaves of high-class sherry from Pedro Domecq & Company on the speculation that the partners and their friends would take up allocations, namely R. Parker, T. L. Wardle, G. Whitehead, G. Gray, C. L. Wood, Charles Newton, Evan Hanbury and W. Wroughton. He pointed out that the cost to the firm was approximately £9 per octave (or 30s a dozen bottles), sold to the customers at £14 (or 42s a dozen bottles). He had picked plated taps to be sent with each cask and charged for. He stressed that it was a special wine for which a wine merchant would charge 72s for a dozen bottles — a golden sherry from the same vineyards as the Old Telford sherry (presumably a dry *oloroso*). To encourage the others, he mentioned that he had already purchased an octave for himself. (An octave is a measured quantity, being one eighth of a pipe or 13.5 gallons.)

Monro questioned the wisdom of the agreement reached with the telephone company on its charges, wondering whether it was really a good idea to give up an exclusive line and yet still pay a rental as if it were.

Monro had been thinking about the Sam Smith offer and set out his thoughts on how to proceed. He suggested that Smith should agree to £40,000 at 4 per cent and that the capital sum should be paid to him in the event of a company being formed, 'and not otherwise'. In these circumstances Smith could lease his properties to the firm for 21 years, and Monro calculated that the rent and interest payable by the firm would be balanced out by the rents they themselves would receive from the properties; the trade in the houses would therefore cost them nothing. He wrote this in red ink, just in case any partner might miss the entry.

He followed this with an injunction to pay mortgage interest on time, as mortgagees depended on regular payments. A degree of self-interest was involved in making this principled statement, for one of the mortgagees was his aunt, Miss Jane Monro.

The New Year filled Monro with energy; he advised the firm to subscribe to the *Wine, Spirit and Beer Review* at one guinea a year; he did so himself and felt the reading of great service.

He inspected the stables with the vet and found that nearly every horse had influenza and that they would be lucky if they lost only one or two. They all had temperatures and were coughing and steaming at the nose. 'We are entirely to blame for this, we are always underhorsed, and there is not a shadow of a doubt, but that Taylor's hireling, the kicking squealing bitch, brought the influenza here – we have always had two or more spare horses than we want, and should *never hire*, except in summer for the camp work.' Monro's style of expression never left any room for courteous dissent, honest doubt or diplomatic compromise.

Tripp returned to the office on 14 January and his first entry concerned the horses; he reported laconically that they were better and that Snarry (the vet) hoped they were out of danger.

He stated that the *Wine, Spirit and Beer Review* magazine had been ordered and observed that it was the only paper that gave quotations of brewery shares.

As for the telephone rent, Tripp stated that another call bell could be put in the office at Tadcaster; the rent arrangement was 'remarkably cheap' and the company 'had met the firm more than liberally'.

On Ashton's problem, Tripp reported that he had seen the solicitor and that 'if the chief constable goes on much longer with his tyranny we shall not be able to find tenants for our houses.'

He reported that Sam Smith had returned the firm's paper with only the annual rent of the houses and a rough statement – 'trade 50 to 60 barrels a week'. The paper was sent back to him with a request for individual house details. 'It looks very fishy if he will not give this, and one cannot estimate a large matter like this without proper figures for a basis.'

He reported that the mortgagees had been paid interest to 30 September last; it was not surprising that they might be concerned. The agent of one of the mortgagees, no doubt concerned about the strength of the security, had asked for details of the rents paid in respect of the houses in the mortgage, which were very much less than the interest payable on the loan. It was decided not to supply this information on the grounds that the agent knew nothing about valuing public houses.

17 January 1889

Tripp visited the Grimsby depot and found trade very good and that the traveller, Thursby, was proving useful. A new dray had been bought – the only problem about it being that 'the Lincolnshire gauge is three inches wider than ours, and hence in the country it is awkward'. He also saw Evison, a large publican and horse dealer, about a new horse suitable for the beer trade in Grimsby at a price of £45.

Having returned to York, Tripp saw the Markets' Committee and agreed to the tenant at Foss Bridge paying five shillings a week to keep the pig market; he could get this sum back from the pigs' totters at 4d a pen – an awkward matter had ended well.

18 January 1889

Ashton's case was heard at Guildhall. Even the lord mayor said there was no evidence and there was general comment that it was a shame the chief constable should have brought the case to court.

Swales, the North Eastern Railway Company's goods agent, quoted special rates for hauling beer to Sunderland to supply Wyeth's Mart Quay Brewery there. Subsequently, Tripp went up to Sunderland and inspected the brewery, which he described as a dreadful place, with no approach and no cellars; visiting his houses, he found them in wretched order; he felt it very unlikely that any business would be done. During that day he also visited South and North Shields, and then went to Newcastle-upon-Tyne and caught the mail train back to York.

Carter's cashier came over from Knottingley and offered £800 for the Lancs & Yorks house. He was told it was out of the question and to think nothing more about it. 'Add £1000 and the firm might start taking interest'.

He noted that the Danubian barley was growing well and making some useful malt and that it would blend nicely with the Yorkshire. All the malthouses were in full swing.

Monro inveighed against a suggestion that a tenant in Grimsby should be supplied with cheap beer for his off-sales trade. What would happen, thundered Monro, was that he would sell it in the house as a better quality beer and ruin the firm's reputation, just as it had been ruined in Yorkshire. Tripp replied immediately that the suggested arrangement was very important to both parties and that the tenant would keep separate books and undertake to maintain his existing trade.

25 January 1889

Pearse, of the firm of solicitors Middlemiss & Pearse of Hull, came over about the purchase of Gale's brewery in Grimsby and was offered £100 as a '*douceur*' if he could persuade Gale to lease rather than sell outright. He wanted that in writing and got it.

30 January 1889

'We are now to have a school board for York – the nonconformists have forced it upon us.' This was a reference to the creation of state schools under the provisions of W. E. Forster's Education Act of 1870, passed by the first Gladstone ministry and funded in part through local rates – hence the indignation. It was 19 years before the act was implemented in York.

1 February 1889

Mr Hotham came in for his rents, due to 31 July 1888! He was promised them by that day's post, with the receipt to be signed and returned. This reminded Tripp to press for the receipt of £925 from the agent, arising out of the sale of the White Swan, York, overdue many months. Late payment of accounts was, even then, a recognized hazard of business.

An analysis of the trade with Collins of Leazes Lane, Newcastle-upon-Tyne, was done. For January the trade was 101 hogsheads; nominally they gave him 42.5 per cent discount, but as they charged him above their normal trade price, the actual discount was 30 per cent. It was considered an extremely good start and Collins reported himself pleased with the quality of the beer.

5 February 1889

Mrs Hainsworth came up from London and brought her son, whom she was to leave as a pupil. She expressed herself well pleased with what she saw and agreed to go over to Tadcaster and leave him with Mark, the brewer. But the same evening she wrote to say that they had gone back to London; she gave no reason except that her son had changed his mind.

A general fear was developing that the firm would not get the contract to supply the Strensall camp in the forthcoming season. It was suggested that they should not begin any work on building stores there and should lobby anyone they knew in authority. They had found out that the new general was against any monopoly supplier.

Monro complained about drays being left out in the open over weekends. He observed three were out at the last weekend. When he asked 'that owl' Shaw (the yard foreman) why this was so, he received the reply that he could not get the drays in by himself, yet he had taken no steps to care for the firm's property – 'he increases if possible in stupidity daily.' Monro then suggested that any drayman who left his dray out at night should be fined 2s 6d, and Shaw fined 5s if he did not report the offence. 'Nothing is so bad for carts as exposure to wet and snow.' He went on to protest about sending the drays over to Tadcaster from York, stating that the firm was underhorsed as it was and that a day's rest would do the horses good. He related that Shillito had come over from Tadcaster that day in deep snow and with mud up to the axles, and that Parker had sent him back again *very* lightly loaded; every journey cost about £2 in wear and tear and this was bad economy. The railway ought to be used in future unless there was a case of urgency.

12 February 1889

Tripp replied to Monro's strictures. It was difficult on a dark night to stow away under the shed, but it would be done if possible. As for trips to Tadcaster, it was a pity to pay carriage on empty casks when the drays were slack. The firm was really quite well horsed and York trade was quiet in January and February. Monro served his purpose though; he kept people on their toes.

18 February 1889

The telephone company asked for permission to put another wire on the top of the old brewery in George Street, York. They were told that they could do so under the same conditions as for the first one. It was to go to Dickinson's in Fulford. 'Ullo' came in for his Christmas box, which was a glass of beer.

It was noted that the new brewing squares and other work had been completed at the brewery and that the new cellar looked splendid; the engines were in excellent working order.

28 February 1889

A note in the diary by Monro said that 'Inasmuch as the action of T. Newton is coming on, surely we should see W. Hotham and *insist* on his sharing expenses of defence, as he is the party who gains everything.'

1 March 1889

A note by Tripp commented on the Newton case. He said that

Badger (the firm's solicitor) had been in the office and had said that it was likely that Hotham would be joined in as defendant with the firm. He went on to say that Leeds must be got home for the trial. He was at present in Australia and well; he left because for years he was surreptitiously married to a lady in Doncaster and had a family. So he left and took them with him abroad.

2 March 1889

Carter & Company raised its offer for the Lancs & Yorks in Knottingley to £1000 and were told – 'no use'.

Trade at Strensall canteen had begun; there were 150 men in camp and they were quite busy. Things seemed more hopeful for the firm. They received a splendid testimonial from Colonel Braddell in Bermuda to help their cause. Tripp went to Strensall at Colonel Smith's request and showed him the testimonial, which was placed before General Daniell. He later heard from Colonel Smith that the general wished Strensall 'to be worked as last year'. So the firm was sure of the trade for 1889, four years running, and considered it very good news.

The City Council approached the firm about selling the Prince of Wales, in Skeldergate, York, for the council wished to widen Fetter Lane. Tripp saw the town clerk and the surveyor at the premises, and the council's finance committee approved an approach to buy the house. The firm intended asking £2500 in view of Monro's mortgage on it for £1780 and its estimated trade value at around £1500.

11 March 1889

It was reported that Saul, the prospective tenant of the Lancs & Yorks public house in Knottingley, which Carter feared would take all their trade, was in the rival's house on a Saturday evening and became involved in a row; he was charged with assault and fined 5s. This, Carter hoped, would prevent him getting a licence. Tripp arranged to acquaint the police with this information.

The Honourable Julian Byng, of the 10th Hussars, called in at the office to enquire if the firm had given any commission to the Strensall canteen accountant. They were truthfully able to tell him that he had not received a shilling. Byng came of a distinguished military lineage and went on to make a notable military career himself, culminating in a field marshal's baton and the governor generalship of Canada.

19 March 1889

A letter was received from Captain the Honourable R. Lawley of the 7th Hussars, Secunderabad, Deccan, India asking if the firm could supply their regimental canteen. The beer would have to be light and consumption would be 40 barrels a month; it would have to be sent at the rate of 20 barrels fortnightly, carriage paid, to Bombay.

The partners wondered if it would be worth their while to start a canteen trade with India and what the cost per ton to Bombay would be. They were aware that McEwan's currently supplied them and that they had raised their prices twice in nine months — hence the reason for seeking a new supplier. It was decided to make every enquiry and to find out present prices.

21 March 1889

Mr James Sully, of 70 Queen Victoria Street, London, called, having come on from Market Weighton. He had a visionary scheme for amalgamating the West Riding breweries, in which Simpson's and others were involved. He said he had £3 million backing and would give 12 years' purchase of any brewery's net annual profits. Tripp thanked him for calling, said the firm would communicate if interested and gave him no information at all.

22 March 1889

They wired India for the price per hogshead paid by the 7th Hussars for ale and Captain Lawley replied that it was 67s. The firm had been gathering information on freight charges and found that those via Hull were the cheapest.

The stalls in the yard of the Five Lions in Walmgate in York had got into a dreadful state and had been repaired at a cost of £70. The partners felt that the firm would never be able to get to the end of repairing old property. So far as this property was concerned, the same complaint was being made by a brewery clerk of the works nearly a century later.

28 March 1889

Tripp had senior non-commissioned officers to dinner to help the canteen business at Strensall. He wrote glumly in the diary that it was 2.00 a.m. before they left, having arrived at 7.30 p.m.

4 April 1889

The partners had a parade of their York-based horses and listed them with their names and duties in the diary:

Jet	black mare, Marshall's mare
Tom	black horse, Malton's horse
Tinker	ditto. Recently purchased, 17.3 high
Captain	ditto. Rawcliffe's horse
Farmer	chestnut, Poad's horse
Ball	brown mare bought from Robson's father-in-law
Jess	ditto, Seedy Joe's one
Belt	light ditto. This one replaced old light cart mare
Polly	brown pony, travellers' etc. pony
Tache	black horse, the one that gets the swollen leg
Royal	chestnut horse recently purchased

6 April 1889

Lord Yarboro sold all his houses in Grimsby at auction and they were all bought by Hewitt. Much surprise was expressed in the town that the firm did not bid and it was reckoned that it did the firm no good at all.

16 April 1889

Every six months a résumé was put into the diary of sales for the period compared with the previous year, with a brief commentary. Sales of beer were up and wines and spirits down; the latter accounted for by a large sale from the Grimsby stores on a clearance basis at no profit. This six-monthly exercise was at the instance of Tripp and a very useful discipline.

The office clerks were required to take their holidays early in the year to be ready for the busy season, particularly the military camps. Thompson and Chapman had already had theirs, and Simpson and Gilderdale were having theirs.

17 April 1889

One hogshead of IPA quality was sent to India via Hull as a trial. A calculation on costing was as follows:

Sale per hogshead (net)	£3 7s 0d
Refund of duty	10s 0d
Estimated expenses	
Cost of cask	£0 17s 6d
Cost of brewing	£1 12s 6d
Carriage to Hull	2s 6d
Carriage to Bombay	9s 0d
Sundries	3s 6d
Net profit per hogshead	12s 0d

They were pleased to have got the supply rights for the York Gala exclusively for 1889.

19 April 1889

The offices closed on Good Friday and Easter Monday, unlike the West Riding where the commercial and practical requirements of the mill owners dictated that mills remained open because boilers could not be shut down on a Friday to start up again on Saturday; instead, Mammon, not for the first time, took precedence over God, but allowed Him obeisance on the Tuesday after Easter *in lieu*. Hence, in the West Riding the Easter holiday was put back and this practice continues even to this day.

Goschen, the chancellor of the Exchequer and the man Winston Churchill's father 'forgot', lifted beer duty by one-fourteenth of a penny, in his own words an 'inappreciable amount'. This was not how the brewers saw it – they filled the correspondence columns of the newspapers with indignant letters and graphic figuring to demonstrated how iniquitous it was; taking into account Mr Gladstone's substitution of beer duty for malt duty at a higher rate, the combined increase was at least 14 per cent. The partners considered what they should do to meet the increase in their costs and Tripp went into detail in the diary to help them. It followed a familiar pattern – reduce the strength of the beer but keep the price the same — the salvation of brewers down the years, at least until recent times when large price increases became standard and the drinking public too numbed to protest. Monro had no difficulty in agreeing the proposals, and the others followed suit.

3 May 1889

Smurthwaite, of Sunderland, came into the office and discussed terms of supply to his houses by the firm; he wanted 55 per cent discount terms, which they thought rather steep, but were quite agreeable to giving 45 per cent, provided they were able to let him have X (one shilling a gallon) and for him to sell it as BA (1s 4d). In the end, they agreed 45 per cent, plus a further 2.5 per cent if the account exceeded £5000 a year, and one month's credit.

4 May 1889

One of the tenants, Gowthorpe, was caught buying beer from Smith. He was told to pay a penalty of double rent within two days or be dismissed.

There was a note in Monro's hand about Saul and the Knottingley house, from which it seemed that Carter had won the battle to keep Saul out as a prospective tenant, for he was saying that it would be considered sharp practice for the firm to keep Saul's £10 deposit when he could not take the Lancs & Yorks house because he had been refused a transfer of the licence. Tripp followed this up with a note that Saul's deposit was legally forfeited to the brewery because he had failed to fulfil his bargain by his own fault, and that the custom of the trade in Yorkshire was to divide the deposit between the existing tenant and the brewery or to pay the valuer's charges out of the deposit and keep the balance, or to keep the lot. It was up to the partners to say what should be done, and they should bear in mind the expenses the firm would be put to by his foolish action. In the end, they gave him back his deposit and the existing tenant would stay so long as he paid £40 within the week. Sadly, Thompson died within a few days.

11 May 1889

Tripp saw Faulkner, the chemist retained by the firm to advise on brewing matters at Tadcaster, who was investigating current problems and tendering advice. He prescribed the use of salicylic acid as a preservative in the beer at a half ounce to a barrel. He also warned that the malts would be poor because of the wet summer in 1888 and that returns would increase. Faulkner's advice was regularly enlisted by Tripp, an innovation brought in by him and a wise one.

C. T. Dundas went off to London for a break; he left his address as 45 Brook Street, Mayfair.

15 May 1889

A complaint was received from Collins, the big customer at Newcastle-upon-Tyne. He had 20 hogsheads which were not bright and were getting old. Tripp went up at once and found that although the beer was only seven to eight weeks old, it was not behaving properly. He criticized the brewery for sending so large an amount all of one brewing. A man was dispatched to Newcastle-upon-Tyne with finings with which to clear the beer.

16 May 1889

Thursby, the Grimsby traveller, was married the previous Monday. 'He seems settled and to be doing well' — it is uncertain whether this was a reference to the marriage or to his activity in the business.

17 May 1889

Monro put a warning in the diary — 'Snarry says don't use green food yet'. It was a reference, not about environmental purity, but about keeping the horses off newly-mown grass, which would give them colic.

18 May 1889

Collins's beer was again bad and it was arranged to bring it all back to the brewery. Mr and Mrs Collins gave warning that it must not happen again. Tripp promised Mrs Collins a sitting of eggs from his game fowls; she was very fond of chicken.

Mrs Putsey, tenant of the Ebor, York, had been allowing her house to be used contrary to law; she was bundled out just ahead of police action.

22 May 1889

Because of the high brewing volumes at Tadcaster, the water supply from the boreholes insufficient and the matter becoming serious, the brewery stopped three hours a day. Briggs, the expert, was sent for and he said the withdrawal of 4800 gallons daily was too much for the boreholes. The solution was to put down another borehole some distance from the present ones, or improve the refrigeration, or be more efficient in the use of water. They agreed to implement the last two recommendations.

A note incidentally recorded Monro's absence in America; it was significant in that both he and Parker were involved financially in investing in brewery companies being formed there, particularly in the Midwest. They were very attractive investments, but rapidly went out of fashion when it was discovered that the dividends were subject to double taxation if remitted back to England. Many years were to pass before the USA and the United Kingdom entered into an agreement on this topic. Parker also had other brewery interests in the United Kingdom and was a director of at least one other brewery company — Yardley's of Wolverhampton.

24 May 1889

Faulkner analysed the Tadcaster borehole water, which he did on a regular basis. It was:

Calcic sulphate (grains per gallon)	15.62
Calcic carbonate	17.06
Magnesic sulphate	14.94
Magnesic carbonate	2.37
Magnesic nitrate	3.33
Sodic chloride	5.20

It was noted that the water was considerably purer than a year ago.

25 May 1889

The chief constable sent a note round concerning Culham, the tenant of the Market Tavern; he was sent for and warned, which was what the chief constable wanted. However, Culham continued in his slack ways and eventually he had to go; the partners then discovered he had pawned his licence!

28 May 1889

Wrigglesworth, the tenant of the Nag's Head, Heworth, left owing £28. Crombie, the solicitor, got £10 from him and an undertaking to work off the balance as a carter in the brewery. They noted that he was 'a strong man, and we shall save a bad debt'.

31 May 1889

Dawnay departed for Mothecombe House, Ivy Bridge, South Devon, for the month of June.

4 June 1889

The extremely hot weather was proving very trying for the beer at Tadcaster. Maule, the brewer, was adjured to keep stocks low and to send out only new beer to the depots and agencies. The water shortage there continued to be a problem. All roofs and windows had been whitewashed to keep out the heat. The new cellar was performing well – the temperature there was just 60°F.

Trade with the military camps spread; those at Stafford, Richmond, Blackpool and Morpeth were being supplied and they were hopeful about Pontefract. The firm worked hard to keep the officers at Strensall happy; they hired steam launches to make trips on the Ouse for them as a diversion from their exercises.

24 June 1889

Having secured a plot of land, the firm had been working on a scheme to build a new public house at Strensall. Tarran, the builder, had prepared a plan of the proposed building, costed out at £4000 plus fitting out. In the traditional response of a brewer, the partners were horrified at the cost and demanded a scheme at no more than £2500. Tarran was used to this, for he produced new plans and figures overnight.

25 June 1889

The chairman of the York School Board, the Reverend Lowther Clarke, had been looking round for sites for new schools and was interested in the Coach & Horses in Swinegate. The partners were not averse to sale and calculated that they would want £800 for it, but asked £900, with six weeks to decide.

26 June 1889

Tarran produced painted signboards for the York Gala – two blue and white, two red and white. The partners felt they should all be the same colour, and those always used – namely, blue and gold.

28 June 1889

It was agreed that a lad was needed in the York office to assist in keeping the register of casks; they took on Auton at 7s 6d a week.

30 June 1889

It was noted that the Tadcaster May rail account was the heaviest on record at £405, reflecting the very good volume of trade being done. The barrels sold in June had increased from 1073 in 1883 to 4119 in the current year, with the York trade shrinking all the time. Business was increasing 'outside and away'.

2 July 1889

Tripp went to Strensall and lunched with Colonel Hopkinson, whom he considered a capital man, even though the colonel said he had never got out of his head or off his palate the memory of the cigar Tripp had given him the previous summer! It had been one of Boly's Monarchs; Tripp felt obliged to send him a box.

4 July 1889

Tripp called in at Earswick to thank the stationmaster there for his help in having Rispin's case at the Flaxton court dismissed, having told Rispin that he must be very careful about Sunday trade (that is, only to serve genuine travellers and not residents). He then saw PC Moll, who had laid the summons, on his way home, and asked him not to be so severe. In the evening, while sitting on the council sanitary committee (Tripp was a city councillor) next to Sir Joseph Terry, a Flaxton justice, he took the opportunity to express his view that PC Moll was too harsh on Rispin.

8 July 1889

Pipe, the manager of the Castleford depot, came over and reported that the public-house tenants were asking for 10 per cent discount because other brewers, such as Bentley's and Carter, were giving it. He was told the firm could do nothing at present.

Smurthwaite's trade with the brewery was very good in the Northeast, and reports had been received that he had praised the beer generally. The partners responded by sending him ten barrels each of ordinary mild beer and the same of bitter ale, to be sold as the better qualities.

This conspiracy between the firm and the customer was an often-used device, the barrels being clearly marked wrongly, and the public upon whom it was visited never seemed to notice the difference in strength of the beers. The brewery could give a large discount and still make a good profit, and the customer could sell on with the same benefit.

9 July 1889

Mr Hotham rose from his sick bed in Fulford and came into the office to collect his rent and interest.

11 July 1889

The partners discussed the proposed new house at Strensall in some detail and, having taken soundings discreetly in the camp, believed the site envisaged would be admirable, near to the station and in the centre of the camp. With stalls for 40 horses and accommodation for several traps, it would be a good letting proposition. But the capital cost blunted their enthusiasm.

12 July 1889

They had word that Newton was going on with his case against the firm and that he had engaged Sir Henry James QC as counsel.

22 July 1889

A letter was received from Captain Lawley in India saying that the trial beers had given every satisfaction. He ordered ten more hogsheads and said that if they gave satisfaction the firm would get the supply.

23 July 1889

A note in a partner's hand asked about insurance for the York offices and spirit stores, 'the stock being so inflammable' – a curious enquiry after so many years. Tripp assured him that everything had been well insured in the Yorkshire office some three years ago.

While the 'away' trade continued to grow, trade in York steadily deteriorated. It was noted that the Leopard in Coney Street took only 1s 6d a day, and the tenant of the Castle said that if he took 10s he was doing big business. Copley at the Spread Eagle in Walmgate was doing next to nothing. It was the same tale everywhere.

25 July 1889

Tripp had one of his regular meetings with the brewer and other staff at Tadcaster. As usual, they pondered long over reports coming in from the hop fields and over the likely yield and price. With the military canteen season over, fewer men were needed and the wage bill had to be reduced.

It was noted that the new railway siding was making good progress and that the new cellar was proving very satisfactory, with the temperature at just 59°F. The ten hogsheads of IPA for India were to be dispatched on Saturday from Hull and were sampled. Returns of beer were accumulating and Maule was told to start blending them shortly. Lastly, there was no shortage of water from the boreholes.

5 August 1889

The partners were considering having electric light at the brewery; the gas bill was now £120 a year – and too much! A few days later they had a visit from Mr Woodhead of Ben Rhydding, the agent for Holmes & Company of Newcastle-upon-Tyne, about installing electricity. He quoted £210 to fix up 106 lights; the only problem was that the brewery had no engine big enough to work the dynamo, nor steam for it. Therefore, it would cost another £90 for an engine and installation. They calculated that in addition to a capital cost of £300, running costs and depreciation would be £74 annually, and that they would save £36 a year over gas. They noted that lamps cost 4s each and would last longer than a year.

Meanwhile, Parker went off to the family home at Shirburn Castle in Oxfordshire, and Dawnay to Danby Lodge, Grosmont.

10 August 1889

The annual brewery outing to Scarborough took place, but it was very wet, which somewhat spoiled the day. However, the men made the most of it and, said Tripp, 'it must cause extra exertions in the future.' They had lunch at the Imperial Hotel in Huntriss Row. When the cloth was removed, the loyal toast was proposed. Mr Buchanan, the cashier, proposed the success of the company and the health of Mr Tripp. He responded by outlining the advances made during the year and observed that there were 20 more employees round the table than last year and said that he hoped (perhaps with inner reservations) that there would be still more next year. A toast was then proposed to the brewer and his staff, followed by one to the travellers and visitors, and finally to 'Our next merry meeting'. Luncheon over, the throng dispersed further to enjoy the benefits and pleasures of 'the Queen of English Watering Places'. Tea was provided and they returned to York by the 10.00 p.m. train.

12 August 1889

It was reported that the 14th regimental depot sergeants' mess had employed a very careless caterer, who had not looked after the beer or done what he had been asked to do. At the mess meeting it was decided to try Bass beer, albeit purchased through the firm; Tripp suspected the caterer had been 'in the pay of someone'.

The partners agreed to buy two acres of land at Strensall for their new public house, at a cost of £200.

The barley-buying season had begun, with the Turkish harvest first in the market; they bought 200 quarters from Keighley, Maxted & Company and the quality was very good. This purchase was to be followed by others, as prices were moderate. As opposed to the previous year, the Yorkshire barley was to prove much better and foreign purchases were greatly reduced, with only Danubian and Californian brewing being bought.

17 August 1889

Tripp left for his holiday in Brighton. Buchanan, the chief clerk, was left in charge, with Tripp's holiday address for emergencies.

Mr Hotham left a message that the firm stood no chance of getting a licence for the proposed Strensall house; he had heard this from Edward Newton. But if the firm obliged Newton he would put them in the way of being successful.

Dawnay felt constrained to complain. The billiard table at the White Swan at Goodramgate in York was purchased for £57 10s 0d. It was hopeless! When they built the room for it, the partners said they would have nothing to do with any table for it. Batty, the tenant, lumbered them with a table, which put up the valuation and then the firm complained it could not get a tenant. It would be just the same with Davy at the Castle, even though it was in writing that the firm would have nothing to do with any billiard table there. A familiar problem – unauthorized additions by tenants to the valuation and expecting to be paid out when they left for items an incoming tenant did not want.

30 August 1889

Parker wrote in his soundings on the Strensall licence application. He was informed that the licence would have been refused anyway because it was felt that the site was wrong, as was the applicant, Taylor. However, it was generally thought that no one other than the firm would get a licence there.

Dawnay could not understand why White had been hired to take two and a half barrels of beer to Riccall when they had four horses in the stable doing nothing and one of the maltsters doing some whitewashing, which could be done at any time. It was felt that since the houses were only some 200 yards from the station it would be better to send small consignments like these by train.

5 October 1889

Parker raised again the matter of selling inferior beer as better beer. He felt that it would not be long before all tied houses would be selling X beer and nothing else – albeit as XXX beer. It was an alarming situation and he went on to say that formerly the firm altered an order from a tied customer to better quality if in their opinion the outlet justified the change. He wound up 'It was always thought and with some reason that cheap beer at top price did harm (i.e. selling X for XXX).' Tripp replied that the reasons for this practice were twofold. First, there was a much greater demand for light ale than there used to be and, second, times were so bad with the houses that the firm was not in a position to interfere with tenants' orders.

Parker put in another regular complaint about the state of the York depot yard, which was cut up and untidy; more whinstone chips had to be ordered.

He also reported that one of the draymen, Hustwick, had been locked up by the police for drunkenness and furious driving. The dray had been led back to the brewery by the police – a public disgrace. Parker himself saw the furious driving and in vain shouted at him in Bootham. He demanded his dismissal. Hustwick was replaced by Richmond from the maltings. In defence of Hustwick, Tripp said he was steady and that his breaking out was strange and disgraceful.

Spirits were delivered to customers in jugs, ranging in capacity from a half gallon to four gallons. Parker had calculated that the number of jugs bought did not relate favourably to the increased trade. Tripp pointed out that the turn round in jugs was at least three months and that, after allowing for breakage and loss, trade was done with a very moderate amount of containers. He pointed out that the cost was charged to profit and not as a capital cost.

11 October 1889

A new boiler was ordered for the brewery at a cost of £385. This would include delivery by the suppliers, Galloways, who would also install it, though the firm would pay for the labour. It was felt necessary to place an order at once, for the costs of labour and materials were rising.

18 October 1889

There was a notification from Somerset House that the firm may not have been paying enough income tax. The inspector of taxes called and had a long chat with Tripp, who arranged to prepare an annual statement of profits since 1883. What caused the enquiry, according to Tripp, was that the brewery companies generally were coming out with large profit statements.

21 October 1889

The partners were very concerned about the cost of engineering and joinery work at the brewery by Messrs Tindal and Outhwaite respectively. They therefore took on an engineer/fitter, Smith, at 35s a week and arranged to buy iron piping and timber directly. Tindal and Outhwaite were to be kept out of the premises! Parker was also still very concerned about the state of the yard. He felt that Tarran did not know the difference between 'employer' and 'employee'. He was conceited and did not carry out instructions – the firm paid the piper and would call the tune.

He was very irritable that day. He complained about the new summary sales book being cumbersome and unnecessarily large. In future, before ordering books, the partners were to be asked for their authorization.

28 October 1889

Tripp saw Tarran and was told that the chips had been on order for a fortnight but had only arrived two days ago. He regretted any mistake and only put down the ballast as a temporary measure. As to the sales summary book, it was upon old lines, but with the addition of the Brigg depot; any special wishes could be attended to.

31 October 1889

Thomas Newton called on Tarran and asked him about the rents of the Wenlock Terrace houses. In the course of their conversation he told Tarran that his case against the firm was going on, and that it made it more strange when Mr Lambton had only just given £20,000 for Mr Monro's share. He went on that he had heard that the firm was doing well. Tarran had told him that it was not so with the York houses, but through canteens and free trade it was improving slightly. Newton then replied 'Yes, I am aware, and how could they expect the York houses to do well when they gave £63,000 for Mr Melrose's houses that are not worth half that sum?' Tripp thought that this admission was important to the firm: £31,500 was half of £63,000, and this sum divided by five (partners), represented £6000 odd off each share, i.e. reduced £15,000 to £9000. The firm had given £10,000. Tarran made a note of Newton's call in his own diary.

1 November 1889

With trade being up, there was a shortage of 36-gallon casks, which was noticed to be an increasingly popular size with customers. Enquiries were made for more, and Robertson & Company delivered 300 barrels at 12s each, compared with Burton suppliers at 21s. However, it was acknowledged that second-hand barrels of this quality were hard to come by.

Mr Roberts (the local surveyor of taxes) from Somerset House had called on the previous day and had laid before him all the figures he had requested, and he seemed, according to Tripp, satisfied with the explanations given. The firm was underpaid in tax for the years 1888 and 1889 to the extent of £174 6s 2d. For the year ended 6 September 1890, the return by the firm of profit was to be £8879 instead of £5250 already declared, and increased tax to be £90. It was considered a very easy get-off, for Mr Roberts would not pass some of the items the firm had deducted in calculating profits.

4 November 1889

A fire at the King's Arms, Bilton Street, York, which occurred on 31 October, caused damage at £7 8s 0d. The London Assurance Company paid out £5 10s 0d on 4 November.

Mr J. McCardle of Dundalk, Northern Ireland, called to offer his firm as agents in Ireland. He seemed to Tripp a very respectable man and enquiries were to be made.

5 November 1889

Newton called in at the office to say that the legal action would go on and that writs would have been issued the previous Monday had Mr Hotham not died.

A further order was received from the 7th Hussars in India for 15 hogsheads twice monthly. Captain Lawley reported the beer in excellent condition, except that there was too much waste while the beer was in transit. He suspected tampering between Bombay and Secunderabad.

6 November 1889

Burke, their traveller on Tyneside, called at the office and (*inter alia*) requested assistance with his rent, as he did not live in a licensed house. This caused Tripp to consider his remuneration, which came out a great deal less than an offer being made to him by a Scottish brewer. Tripp then took out sales figures and found that three of the travellers between them accounted for more than one quarter of the firm's entire trade.

11 November 1889

Tripp noted, as a city councillor, that the Watch Committee had changed its membership. Wrightson and Dodsworth came onto it, and the hope was expressed that it would be fairer than for years past.

14 November 1889

The partners considered Briggs's tender for the new work at the brewery at £5750 to be completed by the end of March 1890.

27 November 1889

Benn, an engineering contractor from Leeds, whose men were repairing a boiler at the brewery, a rush job over day and night, found that they had got so drunk the previous night that they had refused to work again. He had to go to Leeds to get other men, resulting in delay. Benn said that work was so good in Leeds that he had great difficulty in keeping his men.

* * *

When at the end of November 1889 the format of the diary changed from spasmodic, mostly daily entries to weekly set meeting with a fixed agenda of items for consideration, Tripp made an enthusiastic start – the first agenda contained no less than 17 items for resolution. Perhaps his spelling of 'agenda' with two Gs showed a certain insouciance, but it was not picked up.

Tripp had a clear firm hand, but was given to an idiosyncratic approach to the spelling of proper names — Stampford Bridge and Crumbie for the York solicitor, Crombie. He made up the agenda on the morning of the meeting and wrote it into the diary; the meeting was held, and he read out the items one by one to those present and recorded on the opposite page one-line decisions. Interspersed, he continued his daily notes of his activities, but the partners no longer wrote down their views on what immediately concerned them.

The diary became a business-like book and that much duller. For instance, item 5 on the first agenda simply read 'Madras Beer' and the decision 'to send a consignment on trial to Madras'. On the fiery matter of Mr Newton and his lawsuit against the firm, with the involvement of Mr Hotham, simply 'Mr Newton and Mr Hotham', and the decision 'Manager reported Mr Newton's wish to see Mr Hotham'.

Tripp does manage to put in a note that Benn's men were working very badly at the brewery boiler and would not finish it within the week, and that the firm was much inconvenienced.

They had the next meeting a week later; one of the items was a reference to Benn himself being drunk, and the decision that he was 'never to do any more work for us'.

7 December 1889

A report appeared in the *Yorkshire Gazette* on a case against one of the firm's tenants, Thomas Wade of the Turk's Head, King's Court, York, who had been drunk on his own premises.

It was dismissed and the newspaper took the opportunity to pass some scathing comments on the action of the police, and suggested the Watch Committee institute some test by which intoxication might be judged.

11 December 1889

Collins of Newcastle-upon-Tyne, having established a very good trade and credit with the firm, felt the time was opportune to apply some pressure for larger discount terms. Tripp would go to see him within the week. He went up and found it a dreadfully cold day and could not get back until the last train. He settled new terms with Collins, who said he would increase his business from £5800 per annum to £8000 per annum the following year.

He also reported that Mrs Hotham had sent some money to Mrs T. Newton to enable her to go to the south of France.

Trade continued on the up and up; but even the assistance of Auton in the office could not keep the cask ledgers up to date. Tripp felt it necessary to get this recorded in the diary before Parker noticed it.

16 December 1889

Monro's brother was reported to have died at San Remo. The diary carried the information with an exclamation mark. Monro had sold his share in the firm earlier in the year to Claud Lambton, a brother of the Earl of Durham, and his house, Clifton Lodge in York, to Parker. Independent wealth and a passion for horses and hunting took away his interest in breweries. Lambton lost no time in persuading his brother to let houses on the extensive Durham estate to the firm; regular meetings were taking place with Morton, Lord Durham's agent, to lobby for them. Morton was, however, proving elusive by design. Monro and his forthright comments vanished from the pages of the diary.

20 December 1889

It was noted that the firm had sold 50 one-guinea Christmas hampers to date and that they were going well.

26 December 1889

The office opened in the morning for pressing orders and closed at one o'clock.

8 January 1890

With Lambton's assistance and presence, a meeting was held with Morton in the estate office at Fencehouses, about nine of the houses on the Durham estate. They could not be tied for trade until May 1891, but the firm decided to take them and do its best with the tenants for trade. In addition to these houses, there were a further six that had been let.

The trade for December was the largest recorded for the firm.

Despite this, the beer quality was giving cause for concern, with signs of acidity. Faulkner, the chemist, was called in and he advised that Maule had gone wrong in that the new malt was very superior but very fermentable and, with raw grain, had run down lower than it should have, with resulting acidity. He had not altered his brewing plans to cope with it. The solution was to neutralize and prime what was tasting wrong – and for Maule to be more careful.

11 January 1890

Wade, the tenant of the Paragon in York, was behind with his rent and account. The bailiffs were put in and Mrs Wade was sent to the asylum.

Even Tripp was moved to say they were in a sad way. Mrs Thompson, widow of the tenant of the Ebor in York, was felt deserving of the firm's sympathy and help. She and her two children were 'to be seen to, and something done for them, if a home can be found'. Miss Milner was approached and she said she would do what she could.

31 January 1890

Faulkner investigated further problems with the beer. He attributed the trouble to the yeast getting non-assimilative and the nitrogenous matter being thrown out of solution under a catalytic change caused by cold. He advised the use of Bean's grist in place of Indian flaked corn and the system of porter brewing as an improvement on the present way, which was very simple and easy.

1 February 1890

The York Licensed Victuallers' Society was to hold its annual dinner during the month and failing any partner presiding had called on Tripp to do so. It was considered an honour and a useful advertisement for the firm. The previous year Riley-Smith had been chairman. The partners agreed.

5 February 1890

Captain Lawley stopped any further supplies of beer to India for the time being; however, supplies to Madras were satisfactory.

11 February 1890

Tripp went over to Leeds for the Yorkshire Brewers' Association meeting, met Tetley and others, and passed resolutions regarding a reduction in beer duty to be sent to Goschen.

The firm began to tighten up on the tie with tenants. Hitherto, it had been predominantly for cask beer only, with some houses tied for wines and spirits. The policy on renewal of tenancies was now to tie for aerated waters and bottled beers, and this was meeting with resistance. All tenants were told that they either sign a new agreement or get their one month's notice; they all signed. But there was still a long list of tenants not dealing with the firm.

19 February 1890

Maule, the brewer, had been suffering from a series of illnesses, mainly bronchial. He was examined by his own doctor and the firm paid for him to have the advice of Dr Ireland (one guinea) – this was the only recorded note of the firm paying for medical attention to an employee.

22 February 1890

Tripp attended the funeral of Mr and Mrs Myers of Stockton, who were customers of the firm. She died on 13 February and her husband died of grief on the 16th. They left one son (Tripp noted among the melancholy) who had received everything. He would continue to trade with the firm and would, after payment of all debts, have £800 in property.

He went to the funeral, which cost £70; it was the largest Stockton had seen for many years – thousands lined the streets to the cemetery and 130 came back to the tea. Tripp later learned that the son was not legitimate, but the bastard of a duke; hence there was much uncertainty about his inheritance.

28 February 1890

Coates, the tenant of the Castle Howard Ox of York, was caught red-handed buying port and sherry outside his tie. He came into the office and claimed he did not know the firm sold wine; for this lame excuse he was given one month's notice.

8 March 1890

Tripp reported that a conscientious teetotaller who owned the Fishing Dock Hotel in Grimsby opposite the Crown & Anchor, recently bought by the firm for £1280, was intending to close it, which would put up the value of their house to £2000. They were waiting for him to close two other houses he owned in the town. Also, Grange, the solicitor who acted for them in Grimsby, was town clerk and would assist the firm to get a full licence for it.

15 March 1890

Tripp visited the brewery and noted that the extension work was proceeding satisfactorily, although it would not be completed for six weeks yet, despite a promise for the end of March. While there, he heard that Riley-Smith had installed an ice machine in his fermenting room and that his electric light worked very well.

19 March 1890

Tripp reported on the effect of the coal strike. He had arranged with Mr Stobart of Fencehouses to send five trucks of coal to help over — undoubtedly from one of the Earl of Durham's mines.

2 April 1890

The North Eastern Railway Company had issued a 'Notice to Treat' on the firm to acquire the Lord Raglan public house and other property at Castleford. The response was to submit a compensation claim of £6750.

10 April 1890

It was agreed to take on a new traveller for north Yorkshire. Meek, who lived at Dalton near Thirsk, was engaged at a £1 weekly salary (to rise to 30s if satisfactory), plus 5 per cent on all orders and on cash taken, subject to good references.

The rick of hay bought from Spink of Huntington was turning out magnificent; it really scented the stables and the horses were eating it with avidity.

A valuation of the brewery premises at Tadcaster was obtained from Briggs & Company, the brewing equipment manufacturer, for the benefit of the firm's mortgagees. They valued it as follows:

Land	£2700
Plant	£9000
Buildings	£16,000
Goodwill	£13,800
TOTAL	£41,500

Briggs added a rider to their valuation — to a company the worth would be £60,000. The mortgagees, Messrs Lane and Monro, were satisfied, and would lend £13,000 to the firm.

16 April 1890

Tripp explained to the partners that the rearrangement of Gemmell's mortgage would cost the firm £336 in legal fees. The circumstances could not be helped, but he was anxious to point out how expensive it was to disturb a mortgage. Nothing has changed, then or now.

He also reported that bookings of military canteens and messes for the forthcoming summer camp season were very heavy. Also, that the aerated water business was proceeding very satisfactorily and that the increase in beer sales was 'extraordinary'. But this was not as a result of the York tied trade — several tenants were asking for rent reductions and the partners were prepared to consider the requests.

23 April 1890

Tripp reported that the first two shipments of beer to Madras had showed a profit. Also, he had sold 230 barrels of acid beer to Robertson & Company of London at 7s a barrel, and in exchange had purchased 400 empty hogsheads at 19s each.

The firm agreed to a scheme for rewarding the employees who looked after the horses, using funds of £5 saved by the discontinuance of the York Horse Show. There were to be prizes of £2 10s, £1 10s, 15s and 5s for the best-kept horse and harness, with Sergeant Major Crisp of the 10th Hussars as judge.

28 May 1890

After some trouble with the beer, partly because of the onset of warm weather, Faulkner reported that it was due to the inefficiency of the steam, non-purging yeast and dropping beer at the wrong time into the squares below. The whole basic cause was shortage of equipment, which had been rectified. Maule, the brewer, placed his resignation in the hands of the firm if they thought he was to blame. The matter was exhaustively discussed by the partners and Tripp was told to tell Maule he was not to blame, but must be cautious – a curious decision. Collins, at Newcastle-upon-Tyne, the big customer, had declared he had had enough and was leaving the firm. Tripp was visiting him specially to make the peace. The suggested improvements were put into effect and it was reported some ten days later that the beer had never been so good, and Maule stated he now had every confidence. Collins had been visited, and he had agreed to give the firm a last chance.

The North Eastern Railway Company was willing to meet the firm's asking price for the Lord Raglan, Castleford, but not for the adjoining land, which they valued at £800; the firm thought it was worth £3500. Stalemate.

3 June 1890

The teetotallers called a meeting in the Victoria Hall in York to discuss the Government Licensing Bill, which among other matters was proposing to give compensation to owners of closed licensed premises. It was discovered that they had packed the hall with their own supporters by admitting them through a side door before the main doors were opened to the public. The brewers had brought in a speaker of their own from London, named Hadfield, to move an amendment in favour of the bill which, had it not been for the packed meeting and the presence of a large number of women, would have been carried by a wide margin. As it turned out, the teetotallers carried their resolution by a narrow majority.

The trade in general therefore decided to hold its own public meeting a week later in the Corn Exchange in York in an attempt to pass a resolution in favour of the bill. The Country Brewers' Society felt that if the government were not supported by the trade, it would give way and leave the vexing question of compensation to be settled by a future government, which may be less honourable or fair and may even advocate confiscation.

7 June 1890

Mr T. Newton called at the office, saw Tripp, and asked the firm to help him. Gnomically, Tripp noted that he was leaving York.

The firm was discontented with the sugar they were getting from Bostock; it had fallen off in quality and the last delivery was very poor and bad smelling. They therefore proposed to get Garton's saccharine – largely used by Tetley and the best brewers.

11 June 1890

Mr Newton called in again at the office to explain how he wanted the firm to assist him, somehow . . .

13 June 1890

A great meeting was held at the Corn Exchange and carried by a large majority a resolution in favour of the proposed licensing clauses in the government bill. A few days later Tripp went to London, as part of a delegation of six from Yorkshire, to a brewers' conference at the Westminster Palace Hotel, where he met Barclay, Wigan, Bullard, Riley-Smith and some 45 other country brewers. After a discussion for over two hours they agreed to ask the government not to consider any time limit on the operation of the bill (if enacted) for compensation for forfeited licences. They then discussed the matter with several MPs, who received them well and were most cooperative. Wigan was sent for by Ritchie, who talked to him with Mr W. H. Smith and Chamberlain. Exalted heights indeed for a provincial brewer.

25 June 1890

Tripp informed the partners on the position of trade with the military. They had secured the supply for three years of bottled ales, stout and mineral water to most of the army hospitals in the North and Northwestern districts, though their requirements were not expected to be large. Visits to the Macclesfield and Chesterfield depots brought good reports. The militias at Strensall were pleased – as were the Carabineers from Leeds, who were to receive special attention because they had been denied their own canteen because they were only in residence for six weeks. In fact, business at Strensall was so good that extra help was needed, and

June was the best month for trade on record. Fleetwood camp had already promised them its next year's trade.

The extensions at the brewery were proceeding apace after the partners had expressed some disquiet about progress. With the hot weather about to start, Maule was given explicit written instructions on how to act. The beer coming from the new equipment was reported as very good in the trade.

9 July 1890

The increased trade brought office management problems, and to rectify the backward state of the ledgers, Tripp was authorized to take on two more clerks.

Mr T. Newton again approached the firm for help, and it was noted that he had withdrawn all legal action against the firm.

16 July 1890

A large review of the military was held on the Knavesmire in York and, as usual, the firm found bread, cheese and beer for those taking part. Two of the firm's employees, Holden and Gilderdale, were to be married very soon and it was agreed to give them £5 and £2 respectively. The partners also agreed to give £3 3s 0d as a donation to the York Nurses' Society.

24 July 1890

One of Lord Durham's houses in Fencehouses had changed hands and the firm did not have the opportunity to lease it. Mr Lambton was to enquire as to the reason.

3 August 1890

Brooks, a drayman, was drunk and inattentive to duty, and the cashier suspended him. The partners felt that he had had every chance and dismissed him.

18 August 1890

The employees' annual trip to Scarborough was held and it went off well. Riley-Smith was staying in the town and had expressed (indirectly) a wish to attend. The firm decided he should be invited, as it would show friendship and might do good for the future. At the trip, he was reported as having spoken very well of the firm.

Major Manners-Wood for some time had wanted the firm to buy the bandstand of the 10th Hussars and had been told the firm could not entertain the idea on any account. He came to York and saw the partners, and they agreed to do so for the original asking price — £88, and that the 10th Hussars should pay 10 per cent interest on that sum for the use of it.

The lord mayor of York, in his *ex officio* capacity as a magistrate, refused to approve the transfer of the licences of two houses to other sites because the applicants were managers. It was noted that such an objection had never before been taken and it was arranged that the managers should be given tenancies and fresh applications made.

Clipstone, a traveller for John Smith's brewery, made application for a similar position with the firm. Enquiries made about him revealed that he had embezzled £50; he was told his services were not required.

19 August 1890

There was a complaint from Major Gordon from Strensall about the beer — 'he has always been against us.' Tripp reported that all the beer was excellent bar one hogshead, which was thick.

Correspondence ensued with the War Office and matters ended satisfactorily.

Burke, the Newcastle-upon-Tyne manager, reported that some 50 licences would be opposed, with the firm's two tenancies among them. He did not think they would be lost as there was no complaint against them. It was noted that the teetotal party was very strong in Newcastle-upon-Tyne.

20 August 1890

Tripp reported that, because of the rise in value of the rupee, the India contract showed a nice profit and the agents spoke highly of the beer.

5

Losing Interest, 1890–1894

From October 1890 the format of the diary changed again. Tripp ceased to write it up and a new handwriting appeared – in fact several hands. As mentioned earlier, the style adopted was to write items of the agenda on the left-hand page as they came up for discussion and then to write down whatever decision was made on the right-hand page opposite the agenda entry. The names of the partners attending were recorded and the minutes signed by a partner. The narrative became briefer than ever, with very little recorded on an agenda item other than the decision taken; it was thus correspondingly less interesting.

One of the few items on the agenda that might have raised a smile was a cryptic 'Old Bob and Darrell', for which the decision taken was for 'Old Bob to be sold, Darrell to send one on trial'. Incidentally, Old Bob was a horse and Darrell was a dealer. Old Bob fetched £20 10s 0d.

12 November 1890

It was agreed that the partners' attendance fees at meetings were to be five guineas. The meetings were held without the general manager being present.

26 November 1890

The rateable value of the brewery following completion of the extensions was put up from £240 to £720. Tripp was instructed to put in an appeal immediately.

3 December 1890

A suggestion that Lord Wenlock's help be sought about Madras had 'No!' written against the item, but no explanation.

Cryptically, it was noted that Duffin Senior was dead – died Monday at 4.00 and buried Tuesday. Also, Duffin Junior was cut out of the will – 'we cannot advise his taking action one way or other'.

An agenda item 'Suggested letter to the bank re overdraft' – decision 'No!' Apparently the firm had a debit of £10,000.

10 December 1890

Maule left the firm and Alabaster was appointed with a salary of £350 per annum and half the pupil premium, £400 in the second year and £20 towards house rent. He never took up the job, however, for Connett was appointed at £200 annual salary and half the pupil premium, subject to him attending Faulkner's laboratory to learn the slow yeast system.

Mr Owen Tripp was to be the interim brewer until Alabaster arrived, at £3 a week.

17 December 1890

Agenda item – 'Annual dinner 13 January Bassetlaw!!!!!!!' and no other comment.

30 December 1890

Tenders were received for the installation of electric light at the brewery, varying from £880 to £540.

7 January 1891

Collins of Newcastle-upon-Tyne was still pushing for a bigger discount; the partners were having none of it and were standing firm. Several mortgagees on fixed term repayments were not anxious to have their money back, presumably because the interest rate was in their favour. However, it made a source of complaint by the partners over the past ten years turn upside down; hitherto they had been concerned to keep their mortgage money – now they were concerned to pay it off. Even Hotham was insistent on going the full term.

Newton was very much down on his luck. He wrote privately to Tripp asking the firm to lend him £50. The manager was told to reply that they would be inclined to do something for him if he withdrew all he had said against the firm and promised to bring no action against it over his former partnership.

14 January 1891

The partners considered a request to take all the rainwater caught off the brewery roofs. They considered this novel proposition from Copperthwaite and stated that their agreement would be subject to them halting the arrangement at any time if they wanted the water, subject to paying for the equipment.

21 January 1891

The partners considered the performance of Pipe, the traveller, who had been with the firm for six years. They noted his falling sales, deemed him fat and useless, and said that he should be told that his salary would be reduced by £50 unless there was an improvement, and that (regardless of any such improvement) in any case the firm was thinking of a change. He was dismissed before the end of the month.

Newbold, the tenant of the Frog Hall in York, was found with Tetley's beer in his cellar. He was censured and threatened with double rent. Mrs Constable, another tenant, who owed £18 on her account with the firm, was displeased and had referred the matter to Sir F. G. Milner, once a partner and now an MP.

Mr Hotham, while not wanting back his mortgage money too quickly, let it be known that his rents were due.

They noted they had a horse with the staggers. They had no compunction about selling it.

11 February 1891

It was noted in the diary and ringed round with a black line that Mr W. Hotham had died on 7 February, aged 88. The partners agreed with the deceased that rents due to him could be paid six months in arrears, but Mr E. H. Newton, his nephew and heir, at first wanted them when due, but later said he would consider the position.

11 March 1891

It was reported that Lord Durham had no less than 43 houses on his estates in Durham and that the firm had the trade of only 15. Lambton was informed by the other partners that he 'had better see the agents' to remedy this state of affairs.

The firm supplied beer into Liverpool. The Star there was taken into the tied estate and the tenant warned about the back door leading to the lodging house.

The government was getting concerned about the number of public houses being tied for trade by brewers. They had called for a return to be made. The partners commented that such a return of statistics was 'very fictitious' and that the Huddersfield MP had wanted it to see how many houses were tied and free.

19 March 1891

Newton was seen again by Tripp about his rents and he agreed that he would take them with six months' grace; also, that he would take over Hotham's mortgage on an annual reduction by the firm at £700.

25 March 1891

The partners were still concerned about the water supply from boreholes at Tadcaster and were considering sinking another one.

At the Yorkshire Brewers' Association meeting the question of a general election fund was raised and they agreed to donate £250. It was later noted that £29,000 had been subscribed. It was a self-interested subscription – to ensure the support of the government against the extremely active teetotal faction in the country.

They had a census of their tied estate and found they had:

Fully licensed freehold	79
Fully licensed leasehold	86
Beer houses freehold	6
Beer houses leasehold	10
Beer off-licensed freehold	11
Beer off-licensed leasehold	15
Beer and wine	4
TOTAL	211

They were supplying the Royal Station Hotel in York with beer. The porters and cab drivers did not apparently appreciate it – not to their taste – though some five hogsheads were going in weekly.

Pipe, who had been dismissed from his position at Castleford, had taken a house in York and was buying his supplies from the firm. The rearrangement of duties at Castleford had reduced the salary bill from £400 per annum in Pipe's day to £150 per annum, and with the same level of trade.

* * *

Documents for signature on behalf of the firm were now being produced at the weekly meetings and listed. On 4 April a new partnership deed was entered into. Captain Lambton was told that he must pay the legal costs of joining the firm, just as all the previous partners had done.

Hudson, the editor of the *Whisky Trade Review*, wanted to give the firm a 'puff' in his journal. It was noted in the diary that the 'firm would like to be puffed'.

McDowell & Company of Madras had stopped shipments of beer to them till further notice. They wanted the price reducing and a lighter beer to be sent.

25 April 1891

The partners had a modified success in obtaining Lord Durham's houses; they entered into a lease for 21 of them, to be taken over by stages as existing tenants left. To make the necessary deliveries, they would need a man, a dray and a horse, and instructions were given for purchase.

The government's budget proposals were published and the partners noted that the trade would get no redress – only that they were to pay for the free education of the country instead – a reference to the Conservative government's budget proposals from their chancellor, George Goschen, to use the funds accumulated from the increased duty on beer and spirits, intended to provide compensation for cancelled public-house licences, to finance technical education schemes.

An influenza epidemic was raging; nine clerks were ill and

Green, the foreman maltster, died after five days. Tripp was at home with it. Green was buried at Strensall, and Gilstrap & Earl, private maltsters on a large scale, had sent one of their men to help out.

As from 1 May it was decided to use preservatives in all beers brewed, the type and dosage to be administered as directed from the York office.

The Bear's Paw, Micklegate, York, belonging to Mr Preston, of Bootham, who refused an offer of £2300 for the property 12 years previously, was now on offer at £2000. The firm decided to negotiate. Preston also owned the Barefoot Hotel in Micklegate, with a blacksmith's shop, cottage and baker's shop, which was offered to the firm at £103 a year rent.

6 May 1891

A fitter, working at the brewery, suffered a fatal accident, some eight years after a similar fatality.

Scott, now in charge at the Wakefield office, wrote that he was 'very much obliged' for his salary increase. The partners arranged for him to have a telephone.

13 May 1891

At its meeting in Leeds the Yorkshire Brewers' Association passed a resolution 'that all brewers resign any political association'. It was also noted that the chairman resigned on Riley-Smith's motion; quite what was the reason for this was uncertain, as John Gordon, of the Albion Brewery, Leeds, the chairman, had been spoken of in glowing terms and his service to the brewing industry was heartily acknowledged at the annual meeting of the association earlier in the year. Perhaps he was too closely connected with the wrong political party.

The Duke of Portland was building a house on his estate at Ashington, a pit village in Northumberland, and Sir Frederick Milner was asked to see if he could get a lease of it for the firm. Likely trade was estimated at 20 hogsheads a week and rent at £400 per annum.

York County Court had asked Tripp to arbitrate on the rental value of a small brewery at Wetherby belonging to a Mr Coates.

The partners were agreeable to him doing this. It was not an isolated reference to his recognized expertise and he was held in high respect in the trade.

26 May 1891

The brewers at the brewery seemed to be absenting themselves without permission; the partners laid down the law – 'any brewer, first second or third, absenting himself from the brewery for 12 hours at a stretch without due notice to head office York, will be summoned to attend the next meeting of the partners to present an explanation. This applies to foremen and clerks.'

Sir Frederick Milner, departing for South America, undertook to give a power of attorney to Parker and Dawnay to act in his name with regard to all matters affecting the firm.

Lord Downe agreed to the firm supplying the 10th Hussars at their camp at the Curragh, Dublin. If the firm's porter was not suitable then he would accept Watkin's porter bought through the firm.

A harsh world for old horses – 'the old grey horse to be shot'.

5 August 1891

Bromet, the town clerk of Tadcaster, complained that the spent hops from the brewery were making the town drains smell offensive; the inspector of nuisances was being involved. The waste from all five breweries in the town was being discharged into the common sewers and thence into the river wharf, where it fermented and stank – over the years this was a recurring complaint by the few citizens of Tadcaster who did not depend on the brewing industry for their livelihoods. (In fact the situation continued until the 1960s, when the breweries finally paid for a filtration and cleansing system.) The breweries had just cleared up this source of urban friction when they had to deal with the other nuisance of their own making, namely noise. The switch from wooden barrels to metal containers, and the adoption of a 24-hour operation with delivery wagons constantly coming and going, loading and unloading, created a deafening noise. By then there were just three breweries in Tadcaster, two of which were away from the residential areas, but the Tower Brewery, by a feat of town planning, found itself surrounded by new middle-class private houses, almost totally owned and occupied by non-brewery people, strident in protest as only that class can be. Many years and large sums of money were spent on the problem.

12 August 1891

The partners were considering the technical details of installing electric light at the brewery; they were told that arc lights were not suitable and incandescent lamps were better. They were determined to get verification of this.

The firm's coal contracts were due to expire at the end of the month and they were determined to get a better price, offering 6d a ton less for a 12 months' contract.

In respect of the new house they were building at Strensall, the partners were granted a temporary licence to May 1892.

17 August 1891

The employees' outing was to Bridlington — 152 attended — and the men were reported pleased.

* * *

At this point the diary's new abbreviated format became more reserved in style. Items on the agenda were given code names and decisions were cryptically recorded — a far cry from the early days of the partnership, and surprising too considering that the partners kept the diary themselves and that the book was padlocked.

The York justices were still greatly concerned at the number of licensed houses in the city, and were proposing a scheme to refuse to renew 25 houses. The firm sought to raise opposition and was advising breweries involved, particularly J. Smith & Company of Tadcaster, to be legally represented at Brewster Sessions. It was a matter of great seriousness, for the value of houses without licences dropped dramatically and, while it was generally accepted that in older parts of all towns and cities there was a surplus of licensed premises, no scheme was forthcoming for giving compensation to those owners whose houses might be closed for the public good (as some perceived it) but who were nonetheless experiencing hardship trying to run their legitimate businesses. It was not until the passing of the Licensing Act of 1910 that such compensation became payable and then only through a levy on the trade itself.

From the military camps reports came in that the beer was in good condition; even from Madras, for an order was received doubling previous orders – 30 hogsheads every fortnight.

16 September 1891

'Owing to manager going to see what was to be seen in High Street, and going to buy a comb in a 6d bazaar, we may be able to secure 16 houses in Lord Durham's district, and some of the best in the country, one house doing 12 hogsheads a week . . . we have about 45 houses in the Durham district. It is necessary now to appoint a branch agent as the business is increasing so.'

An amalgamation with a firm designated only as 'S' in the diary was being considered; figures were awaited. The next meeting on this matter was held at Parker's house, when it was agreed 'that nothing more could be done unless "S" dropped £50,000 more; also, that the next meeting be a full meeting, and not a "round table" affair like Mr Chamberlain and Sir W. Harcourt' – a reference to the efforts made by the Liberal Party in 1887 to patch up its internal dissension on the topic of Irish Home Rule, the only outcome of which was obfuscation and more dissent.

23 September 1891

Edward Newton warned the firm that the sum of £7000 due to William Hotham's estate might have to be called up; Parker was to see Newton about this.

The balance in the bank account was now regularly being reported and was varying between £15,000 and £25,000 credit.

28 October 1891

First reports received from the accountants showed a very satisfactory year's trading.

18 November 1891

The partners finally accepted the tender of Holmes & Company for the installation of electric light at the brewery at £599 for 191 lights and power for 60 more. Payment was to be £200 three months after completion, £200 12 months after that and the balance two years later again; this was an interesting arrangement for credit compared with the present times.

Parker arranged with Newton that Hotham's mortgage should be paid as to £3150 on 1 April.

PC Alp was considered to be making himself obnoxious. He reported the tenant of the Leopard, Coney Street, York, for permitting domino playing.

21 January 1892

Captain Durham of the 10th Royal Hussars queried the price of stout supplied to the canteen. It was pointed out to him that he had mistaken the price of the cask for the price of the stout. Tripp undertook to point this out clearly but gently to 'the gallant captain'.

27 January 1892

The firm discovered that it had been paying Hotham too much rent under the lease. Also, it was noted that T. Newton had made arrangements with his brother, Edward, to receive £10,000 in cash and £20,000 to be settled on his children. In return, he withdrew all actions against the firm and hoped that the partners would acknowledge him in the street and elsewhere. This was considered to be a satisfactory settlement.

The new well being sunk at the brewery had reached 168 feet and would stop at 180 feet.

A telegram arrived from Madras – 'Please send trial 5 hogsheads stout: sell 48.' The partners thought this was very satisfactory.

3 February 1892

A private letter from Monro was read. The contents were not recorded, but from later entries it became clear that it had been about his loan to the firm of £7000, which he wished to increase to £10,000, on having repayment on six months' notice. The partners were terse and to the point – 'No, certainly not!'

No longer were salaries reviewed each year; the partners waited until applications were made to them for an increase. Sometimes they were granted, but more often turned down; Connett, the brewer, applied and was refused. The partners were irritated by bad beer reports, unauthorized time off and inattention to Faulkner's advice (expensively paid for). It was interesting to note, however, that since he had become brewer at Tadcaster, there had been a significant number of applications for pupillage, though whether this was due to the firm's growing reputation through its military contracts or because of Maule's continuing standing in the trade was not known. He did get his rise in April to £300 per annum and on three months' notice.

The new well at the brewery was taken down to 215 feet, with the water level 43 feet from the surface; water was pumped out at nine gallons a minute for some considerable time and the level fell by 16 feet. It was eventually levelled off at 260 feet in the limestone, where a good supply was found; after three days' pumping a barrel could be filled in 53 seconds.

A well sunk at Strensall to supply the stables went down 151 feet, through rock and sand, and found plenty of water.

2 March 1892

The partners constantly worried about the railway companies' freight charges, and rightly so because they were a big item to set against profit. They ascertained there were regular sailings from Hull to Sunderland and used this knowledge to wring a further reduction from the North Eastern Railway Company's York agent.

9 March 1892

They received legal advice that the overpaid rent to Hotham was not refundable, being out of time for claiming back. They were put out by this advice and mounted a campaign against E. H. Newton to pay them out.

There was an interesting comment in the diary about the accelerating pace of the brewers' tie of outlets — 'Travellers' views of free trade in the future' followed by 'in five years all houses will be tied.'

Charitable donations made: York Hospital £10 (sometimes); soup kitchen £5; dispensary notes £10 10s; Sunday gifts 10s. They agreed to make gifts to charities in York up to £50 per annum. To relieve distress in Teeside they gave £5 for Middlesbrough, £10 for Darlington and the same to Stockton.

An appeal was received from the Durham strikers; no action was apparently taken on it – hardly surprising, having regard to the connection between the mining industry through Lord Durham and the firm through his brother.

Williams, a clerk in the Grimsby office, was dismissed, and no reason was given. He apologized by letter to the partners, who reconsidered their decision at a further partners' meeting and reinstated him.

16 March 1892

Collins, of Newcastle-upon-Tyne, with whom the firm did a very large trade, would not agree to a reduced discount; abruptly they ceased with him – 'finish with him on 1 April'. The monthly bank balance was now regularly in excess of £30,000.

13 April 1892

Leggatt, a new employee, wanted an advance of £30 for the cost of bringing his furniture from London. He might have been expecting a grant; instead, he was advised to borrow from his bank and the firm would guarantee the loan for 18 months.

The Gainsborough Liberal Club returned a hogshead of unfit beer, which was discovered to contain 13 gallons of water and the club was so informed. They thanked the firm for finding it out!

11 May 1892

A fire drill was carried out at the brewery and an inspection showed that all the fire buckets were hung up in the right places and in order.

There was a note for the general information of the partners that '1889 champagne preferred was Mumm, Moët and Giesler.'

30 May 1892

It was noted that the trams passing the Black Swan in Peaseholme

Green in York were damaging the building. Tripp was instructed to write to the secretary of the tram company to make good.

It was also mentioned that the Durham strike still continued; it went on until 8 June.

The long-running problem of what improvements to make to the urinal behind the Leopard, Coppergate, York, still went on. It was all to do with space at the back and ascertaining the property's boundaries. The City Council had served a notice on the firm to carry out remedial work; it was decided to do it and have the legal arguments afterwards.

8 June 1892

E. H. Newton agreed to accept a reduced rent in future to offset overpayment in the past. The lawyers may have had the law on their side but the partners had the influence.

The partners had a cask census – they had 19,000, from hogsheads to sixes – even 504 twenty-fours.

13 June 1892

The firm had a policy of paying a commission to any traveller or agent who successfully brought to its notice any free leasehold house subsequently taken over by the firm. It was decided to end this, for it had been turning out that commission was paid again on the firm buying in the freehold.

They decided that Connett needed careful watching because he was so self-opinionated.

Ice was purchased in bulk from Hull at 15s a ton, with carriage at 10s a ton to the brewery. It was decided to have it always in stock and to order two to three tons at a time.

It was calculated that the brewery could turn out 2020 barrels in six days from 17 brewings. Arrangements were made with other brewers to buy in, if short, on the following terms: J. Smith 35 per cent discount, nine months' open credit (Tadcaster) and to pay carriage of returned empties; Tetley 27 per cent – ditto (Leeds); Sam Smith 33.3 per cent – ditto (later altered to 35 per cent (Tadcaster) and carriage both ways); Springwell 35 per cent – free on rail (Heckmondwike).

It was decided to have no horse parade that year, but to save disappointment among the men, to give out prizes nonetheless. In fact, a procession was held.

It was noted that there had been trouble with the chef they employed at the Altcar military camp; he had been either 'drunk or mad' and was dismissed and a new one appointed. The medical officer at the camp had complained about the beer and had written to the firm; the beer was found to be good and the partners came to the conclusion he had been got at – 'the medical officer's letter game failed this time.' The partners were obsessed, perhaps rightly, about conspiracy and ill-doing so far as supplying military camps was concerned. It was not that simple – the chef threatened the firm with a summons about his dismissal and they felt it necessary to settle the matter with him.

The Royal Show at Warwick was supplied with beer and it was found to be excellent.

3 August 1892

An intriguing item appeared on the agenda – 'Spotted Cow and Privy Council'; the reader might be forgiven for suspecting a conspiracy between State, Church and the landed aristocracy. The matter was rather more mundane. The Spotted Cow public house was owned by York City Council and let to the firm. The toilet facilities were disgraceful and the firm was under pressure from the council to make improvements – which they did with some ill grace.

15 August 1892

It was noted that J. Smith of Tadcaster had turned himself into a limited company – comment in the diary was 'very bad prospectus'.

22 August 1892

Employees' outing to Southport – 'great success in every way'.

The manager reported on his visit to the brewery. The grain drying machine had started up and the foreman's house was being built on a piece of land recently purchased from Brooksbank, on the opposite side of the road. It later transpired that part of the land he had sold to the firm was not his to sell, but was the property of the North Eastern Railway Company, the house being that adjoining the spur leading to the bridge over the river wharf. He gave the firm an extra piece of land in compensation. The house was completed in January 1893.

A tragedy occurred on Skeldergate Bridge in York. A barrel containing 42 gallons of whisky fell off the dray onto the bridge and broke open. It must have been a time of sad reflection and frantic endeavour by those passers-by who liked a drink, and of triumph at the downfall of the sinful by those of teetotal persuasion, of whom there were plenty in York.

29 August 1892

Superintendent Rawlings reported that Darling, tenant of the Hare & Hounds in Riccall, had behaved disgracefully in that 'he drank and went raving mad'. He assaulted the village constable who went to see what the uproar was about, and who reported him for a summons, which was returnable on Brewster Sessions day. The superintendent strongly advised that he should be dismissed, which was done. However, at the hearing of the summons the magistrates found the constable in the wrong and discharged Darling. They recommended that the constable be dismissed from the police force. The police inspector, however, felt that Darling should still be given his notice. Darling came into the office and, after a great deal of talking, was told that the police were 'dead against him' and that he would have to go. In the diary, '*We may have trouble with him*', is underlined. Darling's application to stay was postponed and in the following week petitions were received from the inhabitants of Riccall and Kelfield that he should remain as tenant. The firm still felt he should leave, as otherwise the licence would be jeopardized. Nothing else is recorded in the diary on the affair.

19 September 1892

The old brown horse 'is dead from dropsy. RIP'. This is just about the only sentimental reference in the diary to a horse.

28 September 1892

The electric light is switched on at the brewery for the first time.

Surplus pressed yeast was being sold at £5 a ton delivered to Antwerp; it was calculated at £3 net or £150 annually.

Mr and Mrs Southern, large free-trade customers in Durham, were forever trying to get free gifts. It was agreed to give her a hogshead of stout and £10; her husband a barrel with the wry comment 'shed tears'.

3 October 1892

The partners considered the question of the extract rate, which had been falling for several months, and came to the conclusion that the brewer's carelessness had been the cause of the loss and that he would have to be dismissed. Shortly afterwards they would advertise his position.

10 October 1892

Summonses were beginning to come in about the poor toilet facilities at the houses. A movement was gathering momentum among magistrates that the brewers and owners of public houses should be forced to bring their properties up to date – an ominous trend.

The bank balances being reported were running at between £3000 and £4000, which was an indication that capital expenditure during the summer had been high and, of course, that Newton's mortgage and other lesser charges were being paid off. Trade continued at a good and increasing level.

The brewery entered into a coal contract at 12s a ton, with the coal being delivered to Tadcaster.

A bill for £291 was received from Messrs Leeman, Wilkinson & Badger, the firm's principal solicitors, and the manager was instructed to get it reduced.

18 October 1892

It was noted in the diary that the flood water in York was the highest since 1831 and that they had agreed to contribute to a general relief fund. In addition, the firm would deal liberally with its own tenants affected, bearing in mind the loss of trade. They received an application to subscribe to the society in York for discharged soldiers at £2 2s.

Having had the end of year accounts, they dealt with the annual staff wage rises:

Gilderdale (cashier)	£100 00s	£120 00s
Spence (to take Gilderdale's place)	£68 00s	£80 00s
Brayshaw	£71 00s	£75 00s
Stewart (from 1 January)	£58 00s	£65 00s
Simpson	£58 10s	£65 00s
Auton	£46 16s	£54 12s
Loftus (in charge of wines and spirits)	£57 00s	£71 10s
Dobson	£65 00s	£71 10s
Chapman	£39 00s	£45 10s
Burland (to take Simpson's place)	£32 10s	£39 00s
Cole (from 1 January)	£19 10s	£26 00s
Kew	£39 00s	£45 10s
Thompson	£13 00s	£19 10s
Taylor (from 1 January)	£13 00s	£19 10s
Nutbrown	£13 00s	£19 10s
Branch managers:		
Taylor	£135 00s	£165 00s
Holden	£170 00s	£190 00s
Buchanan	£200 00s	£225 00s

A scheme for overtime work was approved.

21 November 1892

There was a discussion about the trade calendar for 1893 and about how many copies were required. Considered and approved at a later meeting were the usual Christmas presents.

The manager's salary was discussed; it was agreed to offer Tripp £800 per annum with 5 per cent on net profits, after deducting interest on all capital such as loans, mortgages and partners' investments. This sum would be not less than £200. The manager would also get a part of any premium payable by a pupil.

There was consideration of a further list of weekly salaries:

Brackenbury, foreman maltster, from	£2 to £2 5s

Thursby, traveller, Grimsby, from	£150 to £175

Tarran, the clerk of the works, appeared to have a position with the firm that was partly as employee and partly as independent contractor in that he took on his own tradesmen and purchased his own materials. He received £200 per annum.

19 December 1892

Tripp was asked to arbitrate at the request of the North Eastern Railway Company over compensation payable for the acquisition of a brewery and public house in Pilgrim Street, Newcastle-upon-Tyne. The partners agreed.

9 January 1893

It was a fine start to the New Year – the railway company increased its freight charges by 9d a ton. It would cost the firm £500 a year more.

The monthly bank balances were rising again – averaging £13,000.

23 January 1893

The *Geraldine* barge, carrying barley for the firm between Hull and York, sank; the loss was apportioned between the captain, the vendors and the firm equally.

Wood, the agent for the newly amalgamated brewery company at Woodlesford, Leeds – Bentley's – wished to see the firm. As he reported his trade as £13,000 per annum, it would seem he wanted to change his allegiance. It was later given at £6300 and nothing further appeared in the diary about it.

30 January 1893

Connett ceased to be the brewer at the end of 1892 and Rogers took over in the New Year. An item was recorded in the diary on 30 January that if Connett became a nuisance he was to be cautioned not to go to the brewery. The beer was reported to be good under the new brewer, the brewery very clean and the yeast very clear. Rogers was allowed to have a reasonable amount of beer at his house free.

Kilvington, who was in charge of the horses, was considered not to be doing well by them and did not feed them regularly; he was to be warned about his attitude.

13 February 1893

Having received an adverse report from the police superintendent at Heslington, Mrs Hardcastle, tenant of the Charles XII there, was given notice to leave. Mr and Mrs Banks were appointed new tenants (they were reported to be very respectable). The house was to be done up, with two bay windows thrown out and the front cemented, the tenants paying 50 per cent as extra rent.

An extensive order was placed with Briggs, the brewery equipment manufacturer, for new mash tuns, coolers and settling backs, to be installed by 1 April.

The opportunity was taken to consider the design of the firm's cheque book and to approve a new design.

6 March 1893

Scott, the manager at Wakefield, was warned he must not take on leases of houses without the prior consent of the partners; they would rather lose ten houses on offer, than have him decide on his own account. The Quarry, Horbury, taken by Scott for five years at £40 per annum rent, was accepted, but no more.

The purchase by the North Eastern Railway Company of the firm's Castleford property did not proceed in its entirety; the company bought some land and installed a siding to the firm's malting.

The Royal Station Hotel in York's refreshment room for train passengers was being supplied in part by the firm. It did ten hogsheads weekly, the firm having half the trade. Dining cars and toilets on trains were still some distance in the future and the often pressing needs of travellers were met by lengthy stays at principal stations. Hence the good business done in the station buffets and dining rooms.

Legge, from Leedham's Stables in York, was appointed as the new horse feeder at 30s a week. He had to find his own house.

Trade in the inner-city houses in York continued to be very poor. The Five Lions, Walmgate, was let at £65 per annum and, to retain the tenant, it was agreed to give £15 back to him 'till better times'.

Gowthorpe, the tenant of the Marcia, Bishopthorpe, was fined for permitting the playing of cards. It was thought a very serious offence by the partners and he was given notice.

A report was received from Tripp on his activities in attending and speaking at meetings and rallies against the Local Veto Bill before Parliament, providing for local referendums on opening hours for public houses. As if the licensed trade did not have enough with the teetotal faction, it was being assaulted by the moderates as well. Mass meetings were to be held at Leeds against the bill; it was eventually abandoned by the Liberal government, having proved to be very unpopular.

13 March 1893

As part of the installation of electric lighting at the brewery, Hays, the contractor, was to put in storage accumulators (at least, that was the general belief), but no one knew their location. The partners considered the matter and agreed that Hays should be asked where they were. However, it appeared he had not installed them because it was not part of his contract to do so. Tripp was deputed when in London to get details of the best accumulator and returned with the advice that it was 'Lithanode'. An order was placed and they were delivered.

An appeal was received from Castleford for distressed children and £2 2s was sent for a children's breakfast.

27 March 1893

The firm agreed to early closing of the offices on Saturdays for the convenience of the clerks 'for a reasonable time with pleasure'.

For Butler, a clerk at Castleford, however, the partners thought he would be better out of the way altogether and he was given his notice. They were firmly of the view that a man could not serve two masters and decreed that 'no clerk [was] to remain in future in the service of the firm who has interest in any other business'.

17 April 1893

A request was received from Buchanan, the Newcastle-upon-Tyne manager, for a stronger beer, and it was agreed to brew one. This was increasingly demanded in the Northeast from the 1870s onwards, with all brewers catering for this trend.

What was taken for ordinary bitter beer elsewhere would not sell there, and brewers produced a stronger beer as an ordinary bitter, which brought with it the custom of serving it in glasses rinsed first under a cold water tap and then filled to overflowing with the head made up of open bubbles rising in a pyramid, which was struck off with a wooden spatula before serving in the presence of the customer.

Thick glass beer mugs were rejected in favour of thin walled clear glasses without handles and the bars in a busy house would be afloat with beer slops by the end of a session. These customs continued until the 1960s, when hygiene regulations brought them to an end.

Gradually the laws against drunkenness, changing social habits and the increasing popularity of other alcoholic drinks saw the disappearance of strong beer as a standard drink. Those who had seen the former style of drinking in the male-dominated public houses and beer houses in the Northeast, with their primitive facilities, will never forget them. They were in total contrast to the rest of England and Wales – only in Scotland was there a similar culture.

The diary effectively closed with a dismal entry – 'trade outlook bad'.

* * *

From then on the entries in the diary became briefer still and items of interest were rarities. In 1894 Parker, Lambton and Dawnay, following a popular city trend of the times, turned the firm into a limited company and became that company's first directors. The legal structure enabled them to sell shares and to get their money out and into other interests quite easily. They were tiring of the whole business of running a brewery, with its often sordid problems, when there were better things to do with their time.

Tripp had left earlier in that year, to become the general manager of Allsopp's Brewery at Burton-on-Trent, and was replaced by Julius Selke, the company secretary, who had been in the York office since the 1880s.

At this point the diary became no more than a minute book for recording decisions.

Appendix
List of Hotels, Inns and Taverns in York, 1872

Name	*Licensee*	*Address*
Acorn	Wm Webster	St Martin's Lane
Adelphi	Henry Gray	Railway Street
Admiral Hawk	Jonas Dobson	Walmgate
Albion Hotel	John Gibson	Parliament Street
Albert	Henry Ostick	Skeldergate
Angel	Wm Sharp	Walmgate
Bar	James Wake	Micklegate
Barefoot	Richard Dean	Micklegate
Barleycorn	James Knight	Coppergate
Barrack	Issachar Schofield	Fulford Road
Bay Horse	George Benson	Blossom Street
Bay Horse	John Humphrey	Gillygate
Bay Horse	Stephen Walton	Marygate
Bay Horse	James Smith	Monkgate
Bay Horse	James Malone	Walmgate
Beehive	Wm Stables	Peter Lane
Beech Tree	Mrs H. Halder	Goodramgate
Bell	John Cleasby	Micklegate
Bird in Hand	John Brown	St Leonard's Place
Black Bull	Wm Graves	St Sampson's Square
Black Bull	George Seavers	Walmgate
Black Horse	Mrs M. A. Dutton	Monkgate
Black Horse	Wm Lewis	Walmgate
Black Swan	John Penrose	Coney Street

Black Swan	John Taylor	Peasholme Green
Blue Bell	Mrs F. Maxwell	Fossgate
Blue Bell	Jasper Costolow	Walmgate
Bowling Green	Mrs J. Styan	Lowther Street
Brewer's Arms	Michael Myers	Walmgate
Brewer's Arms	Thomas Hill	Tanner Row
British Tar	Wm Fowler	North Street
Britannia	John Blenkinsop	Nunnery Lane
Britannia	Wm Brown	Walmgate
Brown Cow	Mrs M. Perry	Hope Street
Burns	Mrs S. McLaren	Market Street
Castle	John Brown	Castlegate
Castle Howard Ox	Silas Usher	Townend Street
Cattle Market	Wm Chapman	Cattle Market
City Arms	John Seavers	Walmgate
Clarence	George Hilton	Davygate
Clock	Mrs Hodgson	Walmgate
Coach & Horses	Thomas Strangeway	Jubbergate
Coach & Horses	George Houlgate	Low Ousegate
Coach & Horses	Mrs E. Stewart	Micklegate
Coach & Horses	James Allen	Swinegate
Cricketer's Arms	John Ashton	Davygate
Cricketer's Arms	James Hanks	Gillygate
Cricketer's Arms	Richard Letby	Tanner Row
Crispin Arms	Thomas Hatfield	Church Lane
Cross Keys	Mrs E. Mountain	Goodramgate
Cross Keys	Mrs M. Elliott	Penley's Grove Street
Crown	Charles Swales	Holgate Road
Crown	Robert Spence	Hungate
Crown	Robert H. Gicks	Micklegate
Crown	Robert Graham	North Street
Crown & Anchor	Wm Spink	King's Staith
Crown & Harp	Benjamin Carlyle	Holgate Road
Crystal Palace	John Robson	Holgate Road
Dove	Peter Donovan	Jackson Street Groves
Duke of York	Robert Cordukes	Walmgate
Duke's Head	Thomas Dickinson	Aldwark
Eagle & Child	Joseph Fowley	Shambles
Ebor	Wm Hutchinson	Aldwark
Ebor	James Sowden	Church Street
Ebor	John Outhwaite	Tanner Row

Edinboro Arms	George Hudson	Fishergate
Elephant & Castle	George Bramley	Skeldergate
Elephant & Castle	Mrs M. Hyton	Skeldergate
Falcon	Charles Hurst	Micklegate
Five Lions	Henry Schofield	Walmgate
Fleece	Wm Coates	Pavement
Foundry	Anthony Herrigan	George Street
Fox	Mrs M. Ellis	Low Petergate
Friendly	John Ruan	Dennis Street
Frog Hall	John Cobb	Layerthorpe
Gardener's Arms	Mrs M. Sotheran	Marygate
Gaructin Head	John Brown	Low Petergate
George	Richard Matthew Edgar	Heslington Road
Glassmakers' Arms	Thomas Croft	Cattle Market
Glassmakers' Arms	Francis Dalton	Cattle Market
Globe	Wm Thomas	Shambles
Golden Ball	Wm Flint	Bishophill Senior
Golden Barrel	James Foster	Walmgate
Golden Lion	Wm Den	Church Street
Golden Lion	Thomas Parkinson	St Sampson's Square
Golden Slipper	Wright Battye	Goodramgate
Great Northern	Mrs Fawcus	Tanner Row
Green Tree	George Whitehead	Lawrence Street
Greyhound	George Exelby	Spurriergate
Half Moon	Richard Hick	Barker Hill
Half Moon	Mrs J. Whitwell	Blake Street
Half Moon	Thomas Cousans	Trinity Lane
Ham & Firkin	George Marshall	Walmgate
Hand & Heart	Wm Clarkson	St Sampson's Square
Haymarket	Thomas Drury	Peasholme Green
Jacobs Well	Richard Beecham	Trinity Lane
Joiners' Arms	George Fisher	Garden Place
Joiners' Arms	George Curry	Nunnery Lane
John Bull	Wm Merchant	Layerthorpe
Jolly Bacchus	John Cooper	Micklegate
Jolly Sailor	Wm George Woodward	Skeldergate
King's Arms	Thomas Beale	Fossgate
King's Arms	Harrison Towse	Layerthorpe
King's Head	Joseph Sharnston	Feasegate
King William IV	Thomas Cox	Fetter Lane
King William IV	Mrs J. Haigh	Layerthorpe

King William IV	Henry Jackson	Walmgate
Lamb	Francis Press	Tanner Row
Leeds Arms	Mrs S. Hill	Peasholme Green
Leopard	Marmaduke Horsley	Coney Street
Leopard	J. Dove	Coppergate
Light Horseman	Wm Nicholson	Fishergate
Lion & Lamb	Michael Fletcher	Blossom Street
Locomotive	Wm Kirlow	Holgate Road
Lord Nelson	James Schofield	Walmgate
Lord Nelson	Wm Linfoot	Walmgate
Magpie & Stump	John Birkill	Penley's Grove Street
Mail Coach	George Milner	St Sampson's Square
Malt Shovel	John Hoyle	Fossgate
Malt Shovel	Mrs M. Hammond	Little Shambles
Malt Shovel	Benjamin Calvert Boast	Walmgate
Mason's Arms	Wm Storey	Fishergate
Nag's Head	Mrs Smiles	Micklegate
Navigation	Mrs C Foster	Skeldergate
Neptune	Thomas Fewster	Shambles
Newcastle Arms	Wm Price	George Street
Newcastle	Robert Thompson	Micklegate
North Eastern	John Holiday	Tanner Row
North Eastern Refreshment	John Marshall	Tanner Row
Old Ebor	Robert Graham	Nunnery Lane
Old George	Wm Heslop	Fossgate
Ouse Bridge	George Ducket	King's Staith
Pack Horse	Richard Cowper	Micklegate
Pack Horse	Wm Ogram	Skeldergate
Phoenix	Joseph Smith	George Street
Prince of Wales	Mrs J. Wheatley	Skeldergate
Punch Bowl	Wm Wood	Blossom Street
Punch Bowl	Edward Jewett	Lowther Street
Punch Bowl	John Hogg	Stonegate
Queen	John McMomency	Lawrence Street
Queens	Henry Churchill	Micklegate
Queen's Head	Isaac Hudson	Bootham
Queen's Head	Stephen Coope	Fossgate
Queen's Staith	Joseph Bean	Queen's Staith
Railway	John Lupton	Blossom Street
Railway	Charles Precious	Tanner's Moat

Railway	Charles Abbott	Tanner Row
Red Lion	George Humphrey	Micklegate
Red Lion	David Shann	St Saviourgate
Red Lion	George Hudson	Walmgate
Reindeer	Henry Deighton	Penley's Grove Street
Robin Hood	Robert Dempsey	Castlegate
Rose & Crown	Mrs S. A. Shepherd	Aldwark
Rose & Crown	Wm Sturdy	St Lawrence Street
Royal Station	John Holiday	Railway Station
Royal Oak	Wm Shutt	Goodramgate
Saddle	Richard Booth	The Mount
Sea Horse	James Mollett	Cattle market
Shakespeare	Wm Shepherd	Stonegate
Ship	Joseph Booth	Castlegate
Ship	James Whitwell	Skeldergate
Shoulder of Mutton	Wm Hall Richardson	Shambles
Slip	D. Potter	Clementhorpe
Slipper	John Wood	Castlegate
Sportsman	Wm Baldwin	Hungate
Sportsman	Beharrel Charles	Nunnery Lane
Spread Eagle	Wm Dalton	Walmgate
Square & Compass	Daniel MacDonald	George Street
Star	Samuel Abbey	Stonegate
Star & Garter	Jonathan Heyworth	Nessgate
St George's	James Roundell	Margaret Street
Sun	W. Morrell	Tanner Row
Talbot	Gervase Wood	Church Street
Tam O'Shanter	Frederick Crow	Lawrence Street
The Clock	Wm Coleman	Parliament Street
The Grapes	Wm Brummitt	Castlegate
Thomas's	Needham	Museum Street
Three Cranes	George Scaife	St Sampson's Square
Three Cups	John Mintoft	Walmgate
Tiger	Raplh Dean	Market Street
Trafalgar Bay	Miss J. Haxby	Nunnery Lane
Trumpet	J. Weatherill Smithson	Tower Street
Turf	Bennett	Market Street
Turk's Head	George Huddlestone	College Street
Turk's Head	Wm Rickett	King's Square
Turk's Head	Mrs H. Garnett	St Andrewgate
Unicorn	Francis Bussey	Lord Mayor's Walk

Unicorn	Duffil	Tanner Row
Victoria	James Schofield	Heslington Road
Victoria	Shaw Thomas	Railway Street
Waggon & Horses	John Dawse	Gillygate
Waggon & Horses	Robert Fisher	Lawrence Street
Wellington	Lawrence Beeby	Goodramgate
Wheatsheaf	Wm H. Briggs	Davygate
Wheatsheaf	Robert Scruton	Hungate
Wheatsheaf	Robert Coates	Nunnery Lane
White Horse	Solomon Wilkinson	Coppergate
White Horse	Robert Wilson	Goodramgate
White Horse	John Crope	Skeldergate
White Swan	Thomas Foreman	Pavement
Windwill	John Wade Batman	Blossom Street
Wool Pack	George Milner	Cattle Market
York	Philip Matthews	Coney Street
York Arms	George Mitchell	Petergate
York Tap	Benjamin Hopper	Davygate
Yorkshire Hussar	Thomas Broughton	North Street
Yorkshireman	David Rennison	Coppergate

Notes:

1. The above list totals 203 premises licensed to sell alcohol, and assuming the population of York in 1872 was about 44,000, it gives one outlet for every 203 persons. To this figure must be added the beer houses which were not required to be licensed by the justices, which totalled another 41.
2. Walmgate, about a quarter mile in extent, had at least 20 licensed premises in its length, and Tanner Row, half as long, ten.
3. Looking at the names of the licensees, it is apparent they often came from a family in the trade, and also that individual licensees had one or more licensed properties under their control, a practice discouraged by the justices in later years. Apart from the hotels, of which there were then some 14, all the licensees would have been tenants or owner-occupiers. A study of a similar list compiled in 1882 reveals changes in the licensees; very few had stayed in the same premises since 1879, and whilst some had moved to other licensed premises, most

had gone out of the trade, indicating a very unstable situation, both financially and for practical control of their premises.

4. The names of the premises are a rewarding study in themselves, as they reflect the contemporary interests and personalities then engaging popular attention.

List of Brewers and Maltsters in York, 1882

Henry Bentley	Woodlesford, Leeds	depot in York
Brett Brothers	Spurriergate	wholesalers
Hotham & Co	The Brewery, George Street	became Tadcaster Tower Brewery Company in 1882
John Joseph Hunt	The Brewery, Aldwark	brewer
John March	Ogleforth	wholesaler
James Melrose	Walmgate	maltster
William Simpson	Simpson's Row	maltster
Joshua Tetley & Son	Leeds	depot in Swinegate
William & Thomas Varey	Skeldergate	brewers

List of Wine and Spirit Merchants in York, 1879

Brett Brothers	Spurriergate
George Button	Petergate
Cooper Close & Company	Skeldergate
William Cooper	Pavement
George J. A. Farrar	Market Street
George Foster	Walmgate
Henry Gray	Micklegate
Joseph Hillyard	Ousegate
Hotham & Newton	Walmgate
Henry Johnson & Sons	Goodramgate
John McGregor	Ousegate
Maltby Swann	Coppergate
Manstead & Wood	Micklegate
John March	Ogleforth
Mark, Rooke & Sons	Trinity Lane
Charles Needham	Petergate
Joshua Oldfield and George Oldfield	Lendal
J. Pearson & Son	Goodramgate
Melrose & Roper	St Sampson's Square
George Sellers	Fossgate
Robert Simpson	Trinity Lane
John George Smith	Ousegate
W. H. White	Foss Bridge
George Wolstenholme	Petergate
Robert Wood	Monkgate

Banks in York, 1882

Beckett & Company

National Provincial

York City & County Bank

York Savings Bank

York Union Bank

Yorkshire Banking Company

Firms of Solicitors in York, 1882

Henry Walter Badger	Coney Street
Calvert & Fowler	Lendal
William Henry Cobb	Blake Street
George Crombie	Stonegate
W. & E. Gray	Petergate
Leeman, Wilkinson & Company	Coney Street
Munby & Scott	Blake Street
William Phillips	Lendal
Smithson & Teasdale	Lendal

Sundry Names Appearing in the Diaries

Charles Kilvington	stonemason, Hungate
George Acton	auctioneer and valuer, Low Ousegate
George Walker	builder, St Andrewgate
Henry Harrison	land agent and surveyor, Clarence Place, Gillygate
John Kilvington	joiner, Darnborough Street, Bishopthorpe
Joseph Sowray	chemist, Low Petergate
Oldbridge	a small brewer in York in the middle 1880s
Thomas Kilvington	joiner, Jewbury, Barker Hill
Thomas Lambert	ironmonger, Parliament Street
Tonge and Hunter	trustees of the owner of the White Swan, Goodramgate. Tonge was a grocer in Goodramgate and Hunter a furnisher, also in Goodramgate
W. Turner	brewer and maltster, of Gate Helmsley
W. W. & A. E. Hargreaves	publishers of the *York Herald*
William Beckett	banker and MP, York
William Biscombe	builder, Peckett Street
William James	a commercial traveller, Tower Street
William Vesey	joiner, George Street (Vasey)

Index

Index